MACMILLAN/McGRAW-HILL

Math

ESL
Activity Guide

Grade 2

- Unit Planners
- Read Together
- Hands-on Lessons
- Math Activities
- Multilevel Strategies

- Math Vocabulary
- Learning Resources
- Foldables
- Problem Solving
- Assessment

Macmillan McGraw-Hill

Building Math Concepts and Language Skills

The primary purpose of Macmillan/McGraw-Hill Math ESL is to provide differentiated instruction and support for both ESL and grade level math teachers. English language learners will master established math standards at the same time as they participate in the English language acquisition process.

Read Together

Sets the scene to build background and develop oral language by integrating:

- Math Objectives
- ESL Standards
- Reading Skills
- Vocabulary
- Multilevel Strategies

Math at Home

Provides math vocabulary in 3 languages that students can review at home with their families.

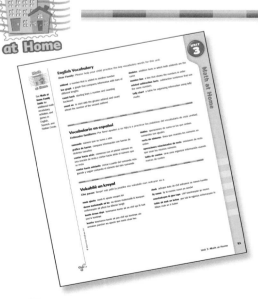

Activities

Each unit contains engaging real-life activities that help English language learners develop and reinforce math concepts.

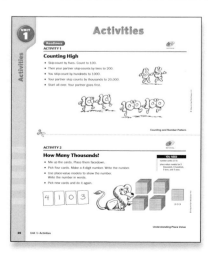

Foldables

Help students organize and summarize math content and vocabulary.

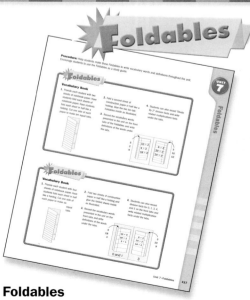

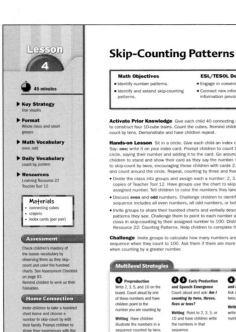

Skip-Counting Patterns

Lesson
4

⏱ 45 minutes

▶ **Key Strategy**
Use visuals

▶ **Format**
Whole class and small groups

▶ **Math Vocabulary**
even, odd

▶ **Daily Vocabulary**
count by, pattern

▶ **Resources**
Learning Resource 22
Teacher Tool 12

Materials
• connecting cubes
• crayons
• index cards (per pair)

Assessment
Check children's mastery of the lesson vocabulary by observing them as they skip-count and color the hundred charts. See Assessment Checklist on page 93. Remind children to work on their Foldables.

Home Connection
Invite children to take a hundred chart home and choose a number to skip-count by with their family. Prompt children to share their experiences with the class.

Math Objectives	**ESL/TESOL Descriptors**
• Identify number patterns.	• Engage in conversation.
• Identify and extend skip-counting patterns.	• Connect new information to information previously learned.

Activate Prior Knowledge Give each child 40 connecting cubes. Instruct them to construct four 10-cube trains. Count the cubes. Remind children that they can count by tens. Demonstrate and have children repeat.

Hands-on Lesson Sit in a circle. Give each child an index card and crayon. Say: **one**; write it on your index card. Prompt children to count by ones around the circle, saying their number and adding it to the card. Go around once more, asking children to stand and show their card as they say the number. Challenge children to skip-count by twos, encouraging those children with cards 2, 4, 6, etc. to stand and count around the circle. Repeat, counting by three and fives.

• Divide the class into groups and assign each a number: 2, 3, 5, or 10. Distribute copies of Teacher Tool 12. Have groups use the chart to skip-count by their assigned number. Tell children to color the numbers they land on.

• Discuss **even** and **odd** numbers. Challenge children to identify whether their sequence includes all even numbers, all odd numbers, or both.

• Invite groups to share their hundred charts and verbally describe the number patterns they see. Challenge them to point to each number as they lead the class in skip-counting by their assigned number to 100. Distribute Learning Resource 22: Counting Patterns. Help children to complete it.

Challenge Invite groups to calculate how many numbers are included in their sequence when they count to 100. Ask them if there are more or fewer numbers when counting by a greater number.

Multilevel Strategies

❶ Preproduction
Write 2, 3, 5, and 10 on the board. Count aloud by one of these numbers and have children point to the number you are counting by.
Writing Have children illustrate the numbers in a sequence counted by twos.

❷❸ Early Production and Speech Emergence
Count aloud and ask: *Am I counting by twos, threes, fives or tens?*
Writing Point to 2, 3, 5, or 10 and have children write the numbers in that sequence.

❹❺ Intermediate and Advanced Fluency
Ask children to count by twos, threes, or fives.
Writing Have children write these numbers using number words.

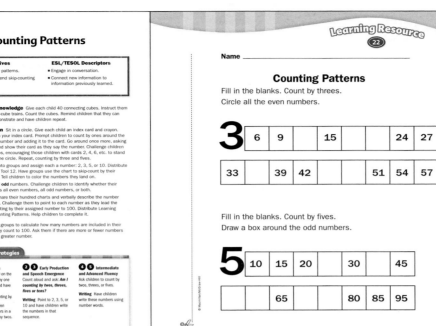

Learning Resource
22

Name _____

Counting Patterns

Fill in the blanks. Count by threes.
Circle all the even numbers.

3
	6	9		15			24	27

33		39	42			51	54	57

Fill in the blanks. Count by fives.
Draw a box around the odd numbers.

5
10	15	20		30		45

		65			80	85		95

Lessons

• Each lesson introduces math concepts by activating prior knowledge

• Modeling opportunities that help students to build math background, master key concepts, and develop thinking skills

• Multilevel strategies, both oral and written, are complemented with a reproducible learning resource

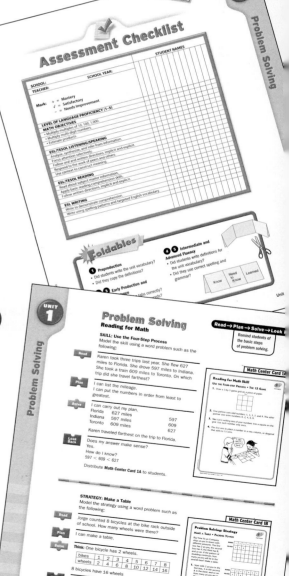

Assessment

• Unit assessment checklist helps teachers monitor and evaluate students' progress

• Foldables provide an additional informal assessment opportunity

Problem Solving

• Lessons use the 4-step heuristic: Read, Plan, Solve, and Look Back

• Mathematical problem-solving models

• Embedded reading skills and math strategies that build reasoning skills

Math at Home
Includes math vocabulary, math-problem practice, and games; in 3 languages.

Math Center Cards
Students come together at the math center and engage in real-life problem-solving situations.

Math Rhymes and Songs CDs
Help develop math concepts and vocabulary and strengthen students' auditory and listening skills.

MACMILLAN/McGRAW-HILL
Overhead Manipulative Kit
Math
Grades K–3

• Attribute Blocks   • Connecting Cubes
• Base Ten   • Counters, Two Colors
• Bills Set   • Fraction Strips
• Clock Dials   • Pattern Blocks
• Cubes

Macmillan/McGraw-Hill

Overhead Manipulatives
Provide teachers with additional resources to model concepts and activities.

www.mmhmath.com provides ESL teachers with additional math resources, such as printable vocabulary cards and ESL appropriate Web-linked activities.

Building Math Concepts and Language Skills

Sally Blake, Ph.D. and Josefina Villamil Tinajero, Ed. D.
The University of Texas at El Paso

The Mathematics Challenge

School teachers are still facing a mathematical problem that is causing great concern: how to teach basic mathematical concepts to the increasing numbers of English Language Learners (ELLs) (Mather & Chiodo, 1994). Most teachers in public schools and colleges are white and female, yet 35% or more of their students are minorities, a growing number of them ELLs. The United States is growing increasingly diverse. The Hispanic population grew more than seven times as fast as other parts of the country between 1980 and 1990 and is projected to double from the year 2110 to 2050, from 39.3 million to 80.7 million (U.S. Census Bureau: 1993).

While some gains in scores of ELLs are evident with national mathematics tests, there still remains a large gap between groups according to scores from *The Nation's Report Card* (NCES 2001). The problem becomes more transparent in the light of international studies. Recent data from the Third International Mathematics and Science Study (TIMSS, 1996, and TIMMS-R, 1999) indicate that US students seldom explore key concepts in mathematics in-depth, that underlying themes and principles are either not identified or simply stated but not developed, and that students spend more time practicing routine procedures than in conceptual mathematical thinking. This problem becomes more pronounced when working with children starting with limited communication skills in the English language.

With this significant and growing percentage of American school children coming from families whose primary language is not English, mainstream classroom teachers must grapple with a much wider range of language development and skill level than in the past. Finding ways to address the needs of students is an ever increasing concern, particularly in mathematics where students experience great difficulty understanding concepts and expressing and exploring their thinking in English. In order to be successful, teachers must pay special attention to methods used to teach second language learners as well as the methods used in the process of teaching mathematics. A school with adequate resources, including teachers, technology, and support staff may succeed well with students whose values and experiences harmonize with the school. However, these schools may be far less successful if the school is dismissive of education that is consistent with students' cultural background (Ginorio & Huston, 2002)

Helping All Children Learn Mathematics

The world is becoming more mathematical and children need more mathematics to survive daily living and to develop job skills for more sophisticated technology. Career advancements and educational opportunities often depend on mathematics achievement. As technology increases, the use of mathematics becomes more important for all people and a part of a social process which people need to understand. The interactions of mathematics and technology and the various fields with human social systems and the values that society applies can influence how children learn and apply mathematics (Johnson, 1989). Answers to mathematics learning questions can no longer be ignored; mathematics is too important of a subject to consider unteachable for any child. Mathematics is no longer a subject reserved for afternoons in classrooms —it is a vital part of life and survival for the modern population. All children must become highly proficient in mathematics.

To become mathematically literate, children must know more than arithmetic. They must acquire knowledge of such important concepts as measurement, geometry, statistics, probability and algebra (Standards, 2000). Educators of children must prepare them for the world in which they will live, one where mathematics is an everyday occurrence not a score on a worksheet. They need opportunities to use number concepts and skills to explore, discover and solve meaningful problems (Gestwicki, 1995).

While English acquisition and literacy development are viewed by teachers as primary goals for ELLs, an equally important objective is engaging students in challenging work in mathematics. Cultural attitudes in the United States make it socially acceptable, even trendy, to lack mathematical knowledge (Deitte & Howe, 2003). This is reinforced when teachers see mathematics as an objective of lesser importance than other subjects. All teachers must subscribe to the notion that all students are capable of and expected to acquire a high level of serious scholarship in mathematics and must offer the core curriculum to all students, regardless of their English language proficiency. In order to accomplish this, teachers must be equipped with the knowledge and skills needed to provide excellent educational experiences for ELLs in math while developing students' language proficiency.

Integrating Language Development with Content Learning

Moreno-Armella, A. & Block, D. (2003) provide evidence that in order to incorporate the immense scientific and technological developments of the past decades for successful school experiences, students must develop the cognitive and academic skills required for learning academic subject matter. Mathematics understanding for children involves many elements. It is a way of solving real problems and of having an understanding of number which includes operations on number, functions and relations, probability and measurement (Brewer, 1995). Students must also acquire high levels of English language proficiency, including the cognitive academic language proficiency needed to manipulate abstract concepts in mathematics (Collier, 1995). To achieve these goals, teachers must integrate language development with content teaching, make use of learner's experiences and focus on higher-level cognitive skills. Instead of seeing language merely as a means of communication, teachers need to see language as a medium of learning (Mohan, 1986).

The challenge for teachers is to identify effective ways in which language instruction and academic content instruction in mathematics can be successfully combined, so as to introduce children to a new language and a new set of cultural experiences simultaneously. The challenge is to adapt the language of instruction without watering down the content and to use materials that follow the core curriculum, but are adapted or supplemented for students acquiring English (Crandall and Willetts, 1986). In order to meet these challenges, teachers must be knowledgeable and skilled at integrating a variety of strategies and techniques that facilitate language growth across the stages of language acquisition while focusing on teaching mathematical concepts. Depth versus breath is an important teaching component of mathematics. Teaching a few topics well is more cognitively sound than teaching many concepts with little understanding. The integration process is important and founded on the following concepts for teaching language and mathematics.

1. The process of doing mathematics/science is not less important than its result.
2. Conceptual learning leads procedural development.
3. It's better to solve one problem by three methods than three problems by one method.
4. The purpose of math/science activity is not to get the right answer but to promote students' thinking. Giving right answers to students is to do their thinking for them.

5. It doesn't matter if you know how to solve 100 problems, it does matter how you approach the rest of them.
6. Do not be afraid of making mistakes but be afraid of repeating them.
7. Fun is a derivative of challenge.
8. What we assess is what we value. (Tchoshanov, Blake & Duval, 2002).

A Conceptually Rich Instruction Sequence is important for all children when learning mathematics. The following sequence is recommended by the Third International Mathematics and Science Study (TIMMS, 1999).

A. Posing a problem/experiment
B. Individual work on the problem
C. Work in pairs and small groups
D. Presentation of the group's solution
E. Whole class discussion
F. Extension and overview of the problem/experiment

This sequence of instruction is also a way to develop language skills and builds confidence in presenting ideas. The process helps students focus on their internalization of concepts, uses discourse with others, and allows reflection.

Facilitating Language Growth Across Stages of Language Acquisition

When working with students acquiring English, it is important to keep in mind that, as individuals, they are at different levels of English and mathematics proficiency. Thus, when planning activities for them, teachers must be aware of the levels of receptive and productive language they bring to the learning task as well as mathematical concepts and skills. There may be some children who are not ready to begin producing oral English. They may be experiencing the "silent period" of language learning during which they listen to rather than produce language although students may have a strong background in mathematics in their native language. The teacher needs to provide conceptual identification activities to more accurately identify children's level of thinking mathematically. Since children's receptive language skills develop earlier than their productive ones (Rice, 1989), it is important to keep in mind that language learning is taking place during this time (Evans, 1990). Children don't always need to respond in order to learn new language skills. They can and do benefit greatly from the opportunity to absorb the conversations of others (Rice, 1989).

Use of Multilevel Strategies. The level of participation and responses required of students during a math lesson can be tailored to address the specific needs of students who may be at different levels of language proficiency. These strategies are known as multilevel strategies. The unique combination of grade-level content plus multi-level teaching strategies can facilitate access to the core curriculum. These multilevel interpretations occur in mathematical thinking and need the same approach as language learners. A pupil's mental development is determined by the content of what he/she is learning (El'koniin & Davydov, V.V., 1975).

Helping Children Move Through The Stages. Students move through a series of predictable stages as they progress towards native-like fluency in English and develop mathematics concepts. Though the stages themselves are predictable, individual language acquisition will vary as students develop at their own pace. Progress along a pathway to fluency is not always signaled by forward movement alone. Rather, students who show growth spurts in acquiring new vocabulary, for example, may exhibit less control in using it grammatically. Such spurts and lags in language development are highly individual and are a normal part of the language acquisition process (Tinajero & Schifini, 1997).

Teachers can create language growth across the stages by using the instructional strategies and techniques discussed below.

Organizing Curriculum for English Language Learners

Teachers must provide English Language Learners with access to the core curriculum in order to help them learn the cognitively demanding and often abstract content in mathematics. Too often ELLs are placed in tracks that do not address the core or main ideas in mathematics necessary for future success. The ESL activities in this guide use the grade-level mathematics content as the vehicle for language development. The multilevel strategies integrated throughout the program facilitate language and content learning. Providing access to a quality mathematics core curriculum is important for several reasons.

1. The core curriculum is consistent with current recommendations from professional societies and research on how children learn. The NCTM Standards, for example, include topics such as estimation, measurement, number, problem solving, spatial sense, patterns, and communication.
2. The core curriculum addresses a broad range of content that is relevant, engaging, and meaningful to all students. This content can be made comprehensible to LEP students through a wide variety of learning experiences, materials and equipment, and ESL instructional strategies.
3. The core curriculum allows for focus on important mathematical topics while integrating cross curriculum areas through thematic/project type planning.
4. The core curriculum emphasizes reasoning, problem solving and decision making essential to success in mathematics.
5. The core curriculum builds the children's sense of competence and an enjoyment of learning.

Maximizing Learning in Mathematics for English Language Learners

The strategies and techniques outlined below are used throughout the ESL Activity Guide adapt, simplify, and supplement the core mathematics textbook in order to make learning more comprehensible and meaningful to students. By incorporating these strategies and techniques, the mathematics content can be presented in a way that is more comprehensible by: (1) contextualizing abstract mathematical problems and activities, (2) effectively combining language instruction and academic content instruction, (3) presenting the mathematics grade level content instead of watering down the academic program and (4) incorporating activities and examples that relate mathematics concepts to the native culture and experiences of students.

Address children's learning from their cultural perspective. Each child comes to school with different backgrounds and beliefs. Children from different cultures and backgrounds should be accepted and appreciated. Activities from other cultures should be integrated with mathematics every day. Teachers must model acceptance of differences and encourage each child to be proud of his or her accomplishments. To increase teachers' awareness of the manner in which they interact with children during the course of the day, videotaping might be used to provide data for self-evaluation of their daily interactions with students.

Provide background experience and personalize lessons. The more knowledge and experience the student has of the language and content of a lesson, the easier it will be to understand it. To make lessons more comprehensible integrate the following ideas:

- draw examples from the experiences of students as the basis for teaching new concepts
- use analogies to relate the teaching of new math concepts to experiences in the students' backgrounds, homes and neighborhoods
- personalize the content by using the names of people and places familiar to students
- use students' names and familiar objects in word problems
- allow students to write their own word problems
- use context or themes with which students are familiar to generate mathematical problems and activities
- encourage students to explain solutions to problems to other students with stronger command of both languages
- simplify English word problems, write short sentences, maintain active voice and use present tense
- elicit experiences and activities that relate to the native culture of the students.

Facilitating Language Growth Across the Stages

When planning lessons or activities, teachers must be aware of students' varied levels of receptive and productive language.

Stage	Students' Behaviors	Teachers' Behaviors	Questioning Techniques
① Preproduction			
■ Students are totally new to English ■ Generally lasts 1–3 months ■ ESL Beginning Level or Pre-literate Level (grades 3–5)	■ Points to or provides other nonverbal responses ■ Actively listens ■ Responds to commands ■ Understands more than can produce	■ Gestures ■ Language focuses on conveying meanings and vocabulary development ■ Does not force students to speak ■ Shows visuals and real objects	■ Point to the __. ■ Find the __. ■ Put the __ next to the __. ■ Do you have the __? ■ Is this a __? ■ Who wants the __?
② Early Production			
■ Students are "low beginners" ■ Generally lasts several weeks ■ ESL Beginning Level or Preliterate Level (grades 3–5)	■ One or two word utterances ■ Uses short phrases and simple sentences related to social, everyday events ■ Listens with greater understanding	■ Asks questions that can be answered by yes/no ■ Ask either/or questions ■ Models correct responses ■ Ensures supportive, low anxiety environment ■ Does not overtly call attention to grammar errors ■ Asks short "WH" questions	■ Yes/no (Did you like the story?) ■ Either/or (Is this a pencil or a crayon?) ■ One-word responses (What am I holding in my hand?) ■ General questions which encourage lists of words (What do you see in the book bag?) ■ Two-word responses (Where did I put the pen?)
③ Speech Emergence			
■ Students are "beginners" ■ May last several weeks or months ■ ESL Intermediate Level	■ Participates in small group activities ■ Demonstrates comprehension in a variety of ways ■ Speaks in short phrases and sentences ■ Begins to use language more freely	■ Focuses content on key concepts ■ Provides frequent comprehension checks ■ Uses performance-based assessment ■ Asks open-ended questions that stimulate language production	■ Why? ■ How? ■ How is this like that? ■ Tell me about __. ■ Talk about __. ■ Describe __. ■ What is in your book bag?
④ ⑤ Intermediate and Advanced Fluency			
■ Students are "high beginners, intermediate, or advanced" May require several years to achieve nativelike fluency in academic settings ■ ESL Intermediate/Advanced Level	■ Participates in reading and writing activities to acquire new information ■ Demonstrates increased levels of accuracy and correctness and is able to express thoughts and feelings ■ Produces language with varied grammatical structures and vocabulary ■ May experience difficulties in abstract, cognitively demanding subjects	■ Fosters conceptual development and expanded literacy through content ■ Continues to make lessons comprehensible and interactive ■ Teaches thinking and study skills ■ Continues to be alert to individual differences in language and culture	■ What would you recommend/suggest? ■ How do you think this story will end? ■ What is this story about? ■ What is your favorite part of the story? ■ Describe/compare __. ■ How are these similar/different? ■ What would happen if __?

Use manipulative materials and hands-on activities.
ELLs need to be supported with hands-on activities that make abstract concepts in math language real to them. Manipulative materials and hands-on activities will help students understand complex and abstract concepts. Concrete materials used in a variety of ways help children represent mathematical ideas. Manipulatives and hands-on activities help students move from understanding simple, concrete concepts to understanding more difficultly and abstract concepts. Activities that involve students actively in solving problems through experimentation, measuring, cutting, charting and weighing are particularly good. Learning centers which provide manipulative materials for exploration and discovery are very effective, as are multi-media materials for learning content and processes.

Plan and organize the classroom to encourage active child involvement and maximize interaction. The most favorable environment for English acquisition is a natural, language-rich setting where students interact with each other and feel comfortable to experiment with language for meaningful communication—much like the context in which they acquired their first language. Students need countless opportunities to hear and use English in small groups and in pairs and to take risks as they try out their developing knowledge of the language and acquire math concepts.

As students complete math assignments, provide them with opportunities to practice their English by increasing the frequency and variety of interactions among students. Pair them with proficient English speakers for math activities such as solving a story problem. Group them with students of varying proficiencies for activities such as measuring, weighing or cutting.

Cooperative learning activities also increases the frequency and variety of second language practice through different types of interaction. Such activities also provides students with opportunities to act as resources for each other and thus assume a more active role in learning.

One of the most important elements associated with successful mathematics learning is the creation of a "risk free" environment where children are allowed to make mistakes without criticism but provided helpful guidance from adults and peers. The children should be encouraged to keep trying and incorrect answers should be regarded as important steps toward learning.

Utilize a variety of teaching methods. Variety addresses not only the needs of children, but the nature of mathematics. Set up engaging learning centers with multilevel activities to address children with different developmental stages and learning styles. Encourage small group work that focuses on cooperative learning to allow for socialization and discourse as recommended by Vygotsky and build confidence in each child's ability to

perform mathematical tasks successfully. The teacher plays an important role in this interaction as a guide for developing and extending knowledge. Learning leads development in mathematics. Encourage peer tutoring–children helping children–to facilitate mathematical understanding. Try team teaching with a bilingual or ESL teacher to increase effectiveness in learning mathematical concepts as well as developing higher levels of language proficiency. Try creative classroom arrangements which encourage talking, writing, modeling and acting out mathematics ideas. Utilize open ended activities in which children solve real life problems.

Develop partnerships with parents and other family members. Outside the classroom, enlist the assistance of parents. Help parents to feel confident that their efforts in the home will help their children do better in school. The home provides the first learning experiences for a child and will serve as reinforcement for what is taught at school. Parents or other family members can encourage mathematics development after school hours and provide valuable background information for the teacher. Helping parents understand how to help children learn mathematics is an important role for the teacher. Techniques such as welcoming parents into the classroom and encouraging their participation in the school program, visiting in the home to establish mutual respect, and communication with the family helps develop home-school relationships. Monthly Mathematics Nights can be planned by teachers.

Integrate the curriculum to build connections between mathematics topics and other subject areas. One way to achieve this is to teach through interdisciplinary projects or broad thematic units. Literature-based units lend themselves to integrated curriculum planning. Some children's mathematics texts, for example, help teachers integrate literature with other curriculum areas.

Allsopp, Lovin, Green, & Savage-Davis (2003) make the following key points concerning learning mathematics.

Teaching in authentic and meaningful contexts. When mathematics makes sense to students or when they see a reason to use mathematics they retain higher levels of learning. This is more important with students struggling with two languages. Making sense of mathematics is a key element in mathematical learning.

Directly modeling both general problem-solving strategies and specific learning strategies using multisensory techniques. The teachers' use of problem-solving strategies and the direct communication of this process with students as the teacher uses it helps students to understand thinking and identify useful stages.

Giving students opportunities to use their language to describe their mathematical understandings. It is emphasized again how important it is for students to be able to use their own natural language to internalize mathematical concepts. False language can develop misconceptions which may stay with students throughout their school career. The internalization of concepts **must** start in the children's natural language.

Providing multiple opportunities to help students use their developing mathematical knowledge and build proficiency. Practice is vital to understanding and gaining confidence in mathematics. Students who may be insecure with their language skills need confidence in their ability to succeed across all learning.

Providing the Right Support with Macmillan/McGraw-Hill's Math ESL

The goal of any mathematics program is to enable children to use math through exploration, discovery and solving meaningful problems based on conceptual knowledge. Macmillan/McGraw-Hill MATH program focuses on these three strategies. The ESL activities in help teachers support the teaching of mathematics to LEP students by providing highly interactive and fun-whole class activities that also address the unique needs and experiences of students. In these activities, ELLS are not isolated from their non-ELL classmates; rather learning is a cooperative venture. And the teacher does not have to

teach the same lesson twice to different groups.

Teaching for understanding and enhancing the process of learning involves holistic skills instruction (Brophy, 1995). In the ESL Activity Guide for Macmillan/McGraw-Hill's MATH, skills are taught to ELLs as strategies adapted to situations, with emphasis on modeling the cognitive components. At the same time, the activities support language development. The suggested activities incorporate a greater range of tasks incorporated in the core mathematics curriculum. As in the core program, the ELL activities allow students to construct their own knowledge in purposeful activities requiring decision-making, problem solving and judgments.

Finally, the integrated approach in Macmillan/McGraw-Hill's MATH allows ELL children to experience cooperative work with others, and time to enhance personal strengths, self knowledge and competencies in all areas of development. Integrated units in the core program address individual learning levels and adhere to the constructivists' theories of learning. As in the core program, the ESL activities allow children learn from experiences, those encountered at random and those to which are introduced deliberately, allowing students to incorporate their own language and cultural experiences.

References

Allsopp, L.L., Green, G. & Savage-Davis, E. (2003). *Why students with special needs have difficulty learning mathematics and what teachers can do to help. Mathematics Teaching in the Middle School*. V.8, 6,p. 308-315.

Brophy, Jere. "Probing the Subtleties of Subject-Matter Teaching." *Contemporary Issues in Curriculum*. (Ornstein and Behar, Eds.). Needham Heights, MA: Allyn and Bacon, 1999.

Clune, William H. (2000) *The National Standards in Math and Science: Developing Consensus, Unresolved Issues, and Unfinished Business.*

Collier, V. (1995). "Acquiring a Second Language for School." *Directions in Language and Education. National Clearing House for Bilingual Education* 1(4) (1995): 1-12.

Deitte, J.M. & Howe, R. M. (2003). *Motivating students to study mathematics. Mathematic Teacher.* V. 96,4,pp. 278-286.

Ginorio, A. & Huston, M. (2001). *Latinas in School. Si. Se puede! Yes, We Can!* Washington, DC: AAUW Educational Foundation.

Kamii C. and Kamii, M. *Negative Effects of Achievement Testing in Mathematics.* Washington, DC: NAEYC, 1990.

Mather, J.R.C. and Chiodo, J. J. (Spring 1994). A mathematical problem: How do we teach mathematics to LEP elementary students?

The Journal of Educational Issues of Language Minority Students. Vol. 13, pp. 1-12. Boise State University.

Mohan, B. A. (1986). Language and content learning: finding common ground. *ERIC/CLL News Bulletin*. Clearinghouse on Language and Linguistics, Vol. 9, No. 2, pp. 1,8.

Moreno-Armella, L. & Blaock, D. (2003). *Democratic access to powerful mathematics in a developing country. In Handbook of International Research in Mathematic Education* (English, L.D., ed.) Mahwah, NJ: Lawrence Erlbaum Associates.

National Board for Professional Teaching Standards (2000). *What Teachers Should Know How to Do.* http://ww.nbpts.org/nbpts/standards/intro.html.

National Council for Accreditation of Teacher Education (2000). *NCATE 2000 Unit Standards.*

National Science Foundation, a. *Women, Minorities, and Persons with Disabilities in Science and Engineering:* 1998. Arlington, VA, 1999.

Reys, R., Reys, B., Lapan, R., Holliday, G., & Wasman, D. (2003). *Teaching and learning mathematics for social justice in an urban, Latino school.* Journal for Research in Mathematics Education. V. 34, 1 p. 37-73.

Rice, M. (1990). Children's language acquisition. *American Psychologist*. Volume 4. February. pp. 149-156

Suter, L.E.(Ed.) National Science Foundation (NSF), 1996. *The learning curve: What we are discovering about U.S. science and mathematics education*. A prefatory report of the National Science Foundation's indicators of science and mathematics education 1995. (NSF 96-53). Washington, D.C.

Tchoshanov, M. Blake, S. & Duval, A. (2002) Preparing Teachers for a New Challenge: Teaching Calculus Concepts in Middle Grades. International Conference on the Teaching of Mathematics Proceedings. Athens, Greece. July 2002.

Tinajero, J. V. and Schifini, A. (1997). *Into English! Teacher's Guide.* Carmel CA: Hampton-Brown Books.

U.S. Department of Education (2001). The Nation's Report Card: Mathematics 2000. Washington, DC: Office of Educational Research and Improvement.

Willoughby, Stephen S. *Mathematics Education for a Changing World.* Alexandria, Virginia: Association for Supervision and Curriculum Development, 1990.

Contents

How To Use | Language-Free Math Inventory

The **Language-Free Math Inventory** assesses the mathematical ability of incoming students at the previous grade level and is taken independently by each student. The purpose of this tool is to focus on mathematics knowledge without involving language. The Inventory assists the teacher in identifying English language learners who are behind cognitively either because they have not had the opportunity to attend school or have not received specially designed academic instruction while learning English.

The items included in the **Language-Free Math Inventory** are based on mathematics standards for students at the previous grade level. The results will reveal who may need remediation. For example, if a student inaccurately responds to or skips two or three sections, you will know where he or she needs help. If a student is unable to complete accurately more than half of the items, you might want to engage him or her in remediation, according to your school's or district's philosophy.

The **Language-Free Math Inventory** is taken independently by each student. All English language learners can complete the inventory at the same time as you monitor them without giving assistance. So that students do not feel overwhelmed, it is suggested that you have them complete one page at a time with breaks in between or over a period of days. As students begin the Inventory, explain that you do not expect them to know how to do all the items and that you will use the results to teach them what they need to know. Try to make students feel that it is okay if they do not know how to do a section; they can skip it. If possible, you might consider communicating the purpose of the Inventory to older students through a bilingual student or parent.

Name _____ **Date** _____

Math Inventory

A. Count and Group Objects

_____

○○○○○ ○○○○○ ○○○○○
○○○○○ ○○○○○ ○○○○○

○○○○○ ○○○○○ ○○○
○○○○○ ○○○○○   _____

_____

△ △ △ △ △ △ △ △
△ △ △ △ △ △ △ △
△ △ △ △ △ △ △ △
△ △ △ △ △ △ △ △
△ △ △ △ △ △ △ △ △
△ △ △ △ △ △ △ △ △
△ △ △ △ △ △ △ △ △
△ △ △ △ △ △ △ △ △
△ △ △ △ △ △ △ △ △
△ △ △ △ △ △ △ △ △   _____

_____

□□□□□□□□□□ □□□□□□□□□□ □□
□□□□□□□□□□ □□□□□□□□□□   _____

_____

B. Count, Read and Write Numbers to 100

1, 2, 3, 4, 5, , 7, 8, 9, 10, ____, 12

45, 46, 47, 48, 49, 50, _____, 52, 53, _____, 55

89, 90, 91, 92, 93, _____, 95, 96, 97, 98, 99, _____

25, 26, 27, 28, 29, _____, 31, 32, 33, 34, 35, _____

Name _____ **Date** _____

Math Inventory

C. Compare Whole Numbers to 100

$<$ $=$ $>$

25 26   69 ◯ 71   86 ◯ 86

18 ◯ 81   35 ◯ 32   59 ◯ 67

D. Count 2s, 5s, 10s, to a Hundred

2, 4, 6, ____, 10

26, 28, 30, _____, 34

10, 12, 14, _____, _____

5, 10, 15, _____, 25

10, 20, 30, _____, _____

60, 70, _____, 90, _____

E. Number Sequencing

5

4• •3 7•   •6

9•   •8
•1
2•- - - •   •16

15•   14 11   •10
        •   •

13•   •12

F. Add and Subtract Facts

−1		+1
4	5	6
	24	
	47	
	69	

−10		+10
50	60	70
	30	
	14	
	73	

Name _____ **Date** _____

Math Inventory

G. Addition and Subtraction Facts to 20

3	6	7	5	10	11	12
+ 4	+ 2	+ 7	+ 6	+ 7	+ 4	+ 6

7

5	6	9	10	11	14	18
– 3	– 5	– 4	– 5	– 4	– 7	– 6

4 + 4 = _____   6 + 3 = _____   7 + 5 = _____   10 + 3 = _____

5 – 2 = _____   6 – 3 = _____   10 – 4 = _____   11 – 5 = _____

H. Add or Subtract Related Facts

| 5 + 3 = 8 |
| 6 + 6 = 12 |
| 9 + 7 = 16 |
| 12 + 3 = 15 |

| 16 – 7 = 9 |
| 8 – 5 = 3 |
| 15 – 12 = 3 |
| 12 – 6 = 6 |

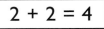

| 2 + 2 = 4 |
| 3 – 2 = 1 |
| 5 – 3 = 2 |
| 1 + 2 = 3 |

I. Extended Patterns

| 1 | 2 | 1 | 2 | | 1 | 2 | 1 | ___ | ___ | ___ | ___ | ___ |

Answer Key

Language-Free Math Inventory

Name _____ Date _____
Math Inventory

A. Count and Group Objects

36

53

87

42

B. Count, Read and Write Numbers to 100

1, 2, 3, 4, 5, **6**, 7, 8, 9, 10, **11**, 12

45, 46, 47, 48, 49, 50, **51**, 52, 53, **54**, 55

89, 90, 91, 92, 93, **94**, 95, 96, 97, 98, 99, **100**

25, 26, 27, 28, 29, **30**, 31, 32, 33, 34, 35, **36**

2   Math Inventory

Name _____ Date _____
Math Inventory

C. Compare Whole Numbers to 100

$<$ $=$ $>$

25 $<$ 26   69 $<$ 71   86 $=$ 86

18 $<$ 81   35 $>$ 32   59 $<$ 67

D. Count 2s, 5s, 10s, to a Hundred

2, 4, 6, **8**, 10

26, 28, 30, **32**, 34

10, 12, 14, **16**, **18**

5, 10, 15, **20**, 25

10, 20, 30, **40**, **50**

60, 70, **80**, 90, **100**

E. Number Sequencing

F. Add and Subtract Facts

-1		$+1$
4	5	**6**
23	24	25
46	47	48
68	69	70

-10		$+10$
50	60	**70**
20	30	40
4	14	24
63	73	83

Math Inventory   3

Name _____ Date _____
Math Inventory

G. Addition and Subtraction Facts to 20

3	6	7	5	10	11	12
+ 4	+ 2	+ 7	+ 6	+ 7	+ 4	+ 6
7	8	14	11	17	15	18

5	6	9	10	11	14	18
− 3	− 5	− 4	− 5	− 4	− 7	− 6
2	1	5	5	7	7	12

4 + 4 = **8**   6 + 3 = **9**   7 + 5 = **12**   10 + 3 = **13**

5 − 2 = **3**   6 − 3 = **3**   10 − 4 = **6**   11 − 5 = **6**

H. Add or Subtract Related Facts

5 + 3 = 8
6 + 6 = 12
9 + 7 = 16
12 + 3 = 15

16 − 7 = 9
8 − 5 = 3
15 − 12 = 3
12 − 6 = 6

2 + 2 = 4
3 − 2 = 1
5 − 3 = 2
1 + 2 = 3

I. Extended Patterns

1 2 1 2   1 2 1 **2** **1** **2** 1 **2**

4   Math Inventory

UNIT 1 Planner

Number and Addition and Subtraction Facts

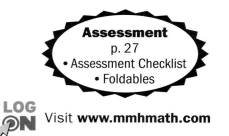

Assessment
p. 27
• Assessment Checklist
• Foldables

LOG ON Visit www.mmhmath.com

Unit Activities	• **Activity 1** Readiness Freckle Faces, p. 10	• **Activity 3** A Name Game, p. 11
	• **Activity 2** Spinner Problems, p. 10	• **Activity 4** Subtraction Race, p. 11

Lessons	Key Objectives	Vocabulary	Materials	Resources
READ TOGETHER "About Feet" by Margaret Hillert, pp. 8–9	**Math:** Count, read, write, and represent numbers in the real world. **ESL/TESOL:** Goal 1/2, Standard, 3/3.	centipede, complete, creatures, feet, insects, poem, quite, score, speed, spiders		Graphic Organizer 1
UNIT WARM-UP Understanding Numbers p. 12	**Math:** Count, read, write, and represent numbers in the real world. Identify number patterns. **ESL/TESOL:** Goal 2/1, Standard 1/3.	counting pattern	butcher paper, counters, crayons, cubes, markers, pattern blocks	Teacher Tools 1 and 2 **Overhead Manipulatives**
LESSON 1 Numbers to 20 pp. 14–15	**Math:** Identify and use numbers. Identify number patterns **ESL/TESOL:** Goal 2/1, Standard 1/3.	counting pattern, skip-count	counters, number name cards (0–20)	Learning Resource 1 Teacher Tools 1 and 2
LESSON 2 Addition Strategies pp. 16–17	**Math:** Add, facts to 20. **ESL/TESOL:** Goal 1/2, Standard 3/1.	add, addend, count on, equals, greater, number line, number sentence, sum, zero	connecting cubes, index cards, markers	Learning Resource 2 Teacher Tool 5
LESSON 3 Add Three Numbers pp. 18–19	**Math:** Add three 1-digit numbers. **ESL/TESOL:** Goal 1/2, Standard 3/1.	double(s), doubles plus 1, make a ten	counters, number cards for doubles, number cubes	Learning Resource 3 Teacher Tool 4
LESSON 4 Subtraction Skills pp. 20–21	**Math:** Subtract facts to 20. Relate addition and subtraction **ESL/TESOL:** Goal 1/2, Standard 3/1.	count back, difference, related facts, subtract	connecting cubes, crayons, index cards	Learning Resource 4 Teacher Tool 5
LESSON 5 Missing Addends pp. 22–23	**Math:** Relate addition and subtraction. **ESL/TESOL:** Goal 2, Standard 1.	addend, missing addend, related fact	connecting cubes	Learning Resource 5
LESSON 6 Add and Subtract 7, 8, 9 pp. 24–25	**Math:** Use 10 to add and subtract 7, 8, and 9. **ESL/TESOL:** Goal 2/1, Standard 1/3.	fact family	counters, cubes, premade ten-frame	Learning Resource 6
PROBLEM SOLVING p. 26 • Skill: Important Information • Strategy: Draw a Picture	Use skills and strategies to solve problems.			**Math Center Cards 1A, 1B**

See **Math at Home Family Guide** for additional math vocabulary, activities, and games in English, Spanish, and Haitian Creole.

English Vocabulary

Dear Family: Please help your child practice the key vocabulary words for this unit.

addend a number that is added to another number

count on to start with the greater addend and count ahead the number of the second addend

difference how many are left when one number is subtracted from another

doubles addition facts in which both addends are the same

fact family all addition and subtraction sentences that can be written with the same three numbers

number line a line that shows the numbers in order

related facts number sentences that use the same numbers and are part of the same fact family

skip-count to count by more than 1 at a time

Vocabulario en español

Estimados familiares: Por favor ayuden a su hijo/a a practicar las palabras del vocabulario de esta unidad.

sumando número que se suma a otro

contar hacia adelante contar a partir del sumando más grande y seguir contando el número del segundo sumando

diferencia lo que queda después de que un número se resta de otro

dobles operaciones de suma en las que los dos sumandos son iguales

familia de operaciones todas las oraciones de suma y resta que se pueden escribir con los mismos tres números

recta de números línea que muestra los números en orden

operaciones relacionadas oraciones numéricas que usan los mismos números y que forman parte de la misma familia de operaciones

contar salteado contar más de 1 a la vez

Vokabilè an kreyol

Chè paran: Tanpri ede pitit la pratike mo vokabilè nan seksyon sa a.

nonb ajoute se yon nonb ki adisyone ak yon lòt nonb

konte nan lòd kwasan kòmanse konte wajoute yon nomb epi ou kontinye ajoute pandan wap konte

diferans se konbyen ki rete lè ou retire yon nonb nan yon lòt

doub se fraz adisyon kote toulede nomb ou ajoute yo se menm

operasyon menm fanmi tout adisyon ak soustraksyon ki ka ekri ak menm twa chif yo

nomb aliye se yon lign ki montre nonb yo annòd

operasyon ki gen rapo fraz matematik ki sèvi ak menm nonb yo eki sòti nan menm fanmi operasyon an

konte pa miltip konte pa nonb ki pi gran ki 1

About Feet

by Margaret Hillert

 30 minutes

Math Objective
- Count, read, write, and represent numbers in the real world.

ESL/TESOL Descriptors
- Listen to and imitate how others use English.
- Focus attention selectively.

Reading Skill
- Compare and contrast.

Vocabulary
- centipede, complete, creatures, feet, insects, poem, quite, score, speed, spiders

Before Reading

Build Background/Oral Language
Prepare number cards with 2, 4, 6, 8, and 100 on them. Explain that you will read a poem about feet. Ask: **How many feet does a dog have? A bird? A spider?** Write *My feet can ___* and ask: **What can we do with our feet?** Make a list. (*skip, run, walk, jump, kick, dance, etc.*) Invite children to help you make a word web on the board.

During Reading

- Read the poem through once as children read silently.
- Explain vocabulary as needed. Hand out the number cards and ask children to hold them up when they hear that number as you read the poem again.
- Reread the poem slowly as children repeat each line after you. Then read the poem in unison.

Phonological/Phonemic Awareness
Draw attention to the rhyming sounds at the end of each line. Say a rhyming word from the poem and ask children to find the matching rhyme.

After Reading

Write *compare*. Ask: **What is the same about the creatures in the poem?** Write *contrast*. Ask: **What is different about them?** Begin with the number of feet they have, then discuss what each creature can do with its feet. (*climb, dig, etc.*) Write the responses on the board. Then give children Graphic Organizer 1: Word Web and ask them to make their own webs.

Art Divide children into groups, assigning each a number: 2, 4, 6, or 8. Ask them to draw a creature that has that many feet and to describe it using a number word in a simple sentence.

Assessment

Observe students' participation as you read the poem. See Assessment Checklist on page 27.

Multilevel Strategies

1 **Preproduction**
Display pictures of various animals and insects. Say: **Point to an animal with two feet, four feet, etc.**

Writing Point to a picture of an animal or insect and say: **How many feet do you see? Write the number.**

2 3 **Early Production and Speech Emergence**
Display pictures of various animals and insects. Point to different pictures and ask: **How many feet do you see?**

Writing Point to different pictures. Say: **How many feet do you see?** Encourage children to write the answer.

4 5 **Intermediate and Advanced Fluency**
Say: **Choose two animals or insects and tell me what is the same about them.**

Writing Say: **Choose two animals or insects and write ways they are different.**

About Feet

by Margaret Hillert

*How many feet
do these creatures need?*

The centipede is not complete

Unless he has one hundred feet.

Spiders must have eight for speed,

And six is what all insects need.

Other creatures by the score

Cannot do with less than four.

But two are quite enough, you know,

To take me where I want to go.

Activities

Readiness

ACTIVITY 1

INDIVIDUAL

Freckle Faces

Draw four faces on a piece of paper.

YOU NEED
number cube (1–6)
drawing paper

- Roll the number cube. Draw this number of dots on one side of a face.

- Roll the number cube again. Draw this number of dots on the other side.

- Write an addition sentence for the dots on two sides of the face.

- Do it again for the other three faces.

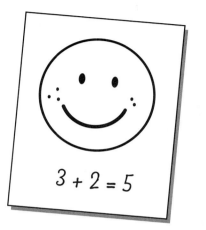

$3 + 2 = 5$

© Macmillan/McGraw-Hill

Read, Write, and Represent Numbers

ACTIVITY 2

PARTNERS

Spinner Problems

Take turns.

YOU NEED
2

- Spin each spinner.

- Use these numbers to write an addition problem.

- Ask your partner to solve the problem.

- Check your partner's answer.

© Macmillan/McGraw-Hill

Add Facts to 20

ACTIVITY 3

PARTNERS

A Name Game

There are ☐ names.

50 ◯

Each name has ◯ letters.

How many letters are there in all?

- Fill in the box with 1, 2, or 3.
  Fill in the circle with 3, 4, or 5.

- Your partner solves the problem.
  Use counters to help.
  Together, write the names that fit
  the problem.

- Play again. Take turns.

Tosha	Greta	David
Ben	Cora	Sue
Lou	Huck	Kenya
Josh	Amy	Merle
Tía	Gail	John

Demonstrate the Meaning of Addition

PARTNERS

ACTIVITY 4

Subtraction Race

Put the cards in a pile on the table. Draw a track like
the one below with 25 spaces from start to finish.
Take turns.

number cards

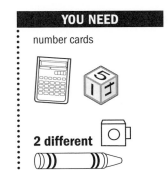

2 different

- Pick 2 cards from the pile. Subtract the smaller
  number from the greater number. Write the
  problem and answer.

- Your partner checks your answer with the
  calculator. If you are right, roll the number cube.
  Move forward that many spaces.

The first player to reach the finish line wins!

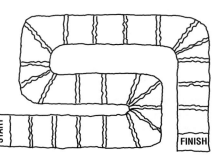

Subtract Facts to 20

Understanding Numbers

 30 minutes

▶ **Key Strategy**
Use visuals

▶ **Format**
Whole class, small groups, and student pairs

▶ **Math Vocabulary**
counting pattern

▶ **Daily Vocabulary**
animals, fewer, more, numbers, zoo

▶ **Resources**
Teacher Tools 1 and 2

▶ **Materials**
butcher paper, counters, crayons, cubes, markers, pattern blocks

Math Objectives	ESL/TESOL Descriptors
▪ Count, read, write, and represent numbers in the real world. ▪ Identify number patterns.	▪ Participate in full class, group, and pair discussions. ▪ Use context to construct meaning.

Activate Prior Knowledge Hold up number cards 1–12, and have children say the numbers with you. Put the cards on the table with 8 crayons, 12 cubes, 9 counters, and 6 pattern blocks. Ask: *How many crayons are on the table?* Ask children to count, find the number card, and hold it up. Continue until children are comfortable counting to 12.

Hands-on Lesson

● Say: *We use numbers every day—to set the alarm, to get on the right bus, to know when it's a birthday, etc.* Invite children to think of school examples. Then ask: *What can we count in the classroom? How many desks are there? How many chairs?* and so on. Count together, then ask: *What counting pattern did we use to count? (ones)*

● Hand out large pieces of paper and crayons to small groups. Invite children to draw a picture about zoo animals that includes things to count. Display and discuss the drawings. Encourage counting opportunities wherever possible.

● Ask questions, such as: *How many animals are in this picture? How many people?* Point to two different pictures; ask: *Which drawing has more animals? Which drawing has fewer animals?*

Challenge Ask pairs to make up a word problem about a zoo animal.

Multilevel Strategies

1 Preproduction
Invite children to point to a zoo picture that shows various numbers of animals. For example: *Point to a picture with 3 elephants (or 3 animals).*

Writing Ask children to write the number of animals.

2 3 Early Production and Speech Emergence
Point to one of the zoo pictures, and ask children to count how many animals are in the picture.

Writing Ask children to write a sentence that includes the number of animals.

4 5 Intermediate and Advanced Fluency
Ask children to choose a zoo picture and describe it.

Writing Ask children to write a description of a zoo picture so that someone else could picture it in their mind.

 LOG ON Visit **www.mmhmath.com** to find printable **Vocabulary Cards** that help build academic language.

Procedure: Help children make these Foldables to write vocabulary words and definitions throughout the unit. Encourage children to use the Foldables as a study guide.

Layered-Look Book

1. Provide each child with two sheets of 11" × 17" paper or use two 6-foot-long sheets of bulletin-board paper to make one large classroom Layered-Look Book.

2. Place the sheets of paper an equal distance apart as illustrated.

3. Roll the bottom of the two sheets up to make 3 tabs the same size. Fold, glue, staple, and label as shown.

4. Have children write math words, symbols, and examples of number relationships under the tabs.

> Exploring Number Relationships
> Numbers
> Number Problems
> Understand Addition and Subtraction

Going Further Children can use the Layered-Look Book to review by comparing their pictures and examples of number relationships.

Folded Chart

1. Fold a sheet of 11" × 17" or 12" × 18" paper in half like a hot dog.

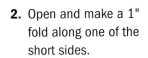

2. Open and make a 1" fold along one of the short sides.

3. Trace along the fold lines to make a chart with two columns.

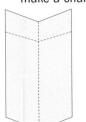 

4. Children can make as many charts as needed to work through the lessons. Teach children how to make their own charts and use them to demonstrate subtraction.

5. Children may want to draw a picture to represent subtraction patterns and write out the names of numbers to reinforce skills.

6. They can also use this drawing to identify missing numbers in patterns.

Going Further Children can use their Folded Charts to review by comparing and contrasting the different strategies presented throughout the lessons. Children can also play an apple toss game to relate addition and subtraction properties.

Number	Subtract All

Number	Subtract Zero

Number	Count back to Subtract

45 minutes

▶ **Key Strategy**
Use manipulatives

▶ **Format**
Whole class and student pairs

▶ **Math Vocabulary**
counting pattern, skip-count

▶ **Daily Vocabulary**
number names (zero to twenty), predict

▶ **Resources**
Learning Resource 1
Teacher Tools 1 and 2

Materials
• counters
• number word cards (0–20)

Assessment

Check children's mastery of the lesson vocabulary by observing them as they complete the lesson. See page 27 for Assessment Checklist.

Home Connection

Ask children to take home their Learning Resource page to show family members. Encourage children to work with a family member counting objects to 20.

Numbers to 20

Math Objectives	**ESL/TESOL Descriptors**
■ Identify and use numbers.	■ Follow oral and written directions.
■ Identify number patterns.	■ Practice new language.

Activate Prior Knowledge Hand out 20 counters to pairs. Write a number between 0 and 20. Ask: *What is this number?* Ask one child to count while the other moves the counters. Repeat, with children reversing roles. Next, display word cards for 0–20. Write each numeral and ask a child to find the word card.

Hands-on Lesson Put 100 counters on a table. Ask children to count them with you. Ask: *Is there a faster way to count large groups by using* counting patterns? *(skip-counting)*

• Write *skip-count.* Elicit different ways to skip-count to 100. *(by twos, fives, and tens)* Ask children to predict which way is the fastest. *(by tens)* Ask a volunteer to group the counters by twos. Count them in unison as you point to each group.

• Have a child group the counters by fives. Count in unison as you point to each group. Then do the activity with groups of ten. Ask: *Which way was the fastest?* *(skip-counting by tens)* **Why?** *(More counters in each group make fewer groups to count.)*

• Hand out number cards and word cards to pairs. Play: "Show Me the Number!" One child shows a number card and says: "Show me (number)." The other child finds the word card and says: "This is the word for (number)."

• Review new math vocabulary, using name cards for numbers, along with the Glossary on page 160. Then distribute Learning Resource 1: Number Name Game! for children to complete on their own.

Cultural Link Invite children to share number songs in their native languages.

Multilevel Strategies

1 Preproduction
Pass out the number and word cards. Say a number and ask children to hold up the cards.

Writing Write a numeral between 0–20 on the board, and have children write the corresponding word.

2 3 Early Production and Speech Emergence
Pass out the number and word cards. Ask children to hold up their cards in order and say them.

Writing Ask children to write the word names for the numerals 1–5.

4 5 Intermediate and Advanced Fluency
Ask children to count aloud to 20.

Writing Ask children to write the word names for numerals 1–20.

Name _____

Number Name Game!

How many? Write the number and the number word.

1.  _____ _____   2. _____ _____

3. _____ _____   4. _____ _____

5. _____ _____   6. _____ _____

Lesson

2

45 minutes

▶ **Key Strategy**
Use manipulatives

▶ **Format**
Whole class and student pairs

▶ **Math Vocabulary**
add, addend, count on, equals, greater, number line, number sentence, sum, zero

▶ **Daily Vocabulary**
order, plus, turn around

▶ **Resources**
Learning Resource 2
Teacher Tool 5

Materials
- connecting cubes
- index cards
- markers

Assessment

Check children's mastery of the lesson vocabulary by observing them as they complete the lesson. See Assessment Checklist on page 27.

Home Connection

Have children take home their Learning Resource page to share. Ask children to work with a family member to write other number sentences and share them with the class.

Addition Strategies

Math Objective	**ESL/TESOL Descriptors**
■ Add, facts to 20.	■ Use context to construct meaning. ■ Follow oral and written directions.

Activate Prior Knowledge Ask children to guess what you are doing as you slowly draw a **number line** to 12. Once they have guessed, write **number line**. Ask children what they know about number lines. Tell them they will learn more about how to use a number line to add.

Hands-on Lesson Show children four red and three yellow cubes. Ask: *How can you* **add** *these two groups?* (count on three cubes to find the total) Count on three using the **number line**. Say: *I start with the greater number, 4, and count on 3. The sum is 7. Write the number sentence 4 + 3 = 7.* Ask: *If you turn around the numbers, which are called* **addends**, *will the sum be the same?* (yes) Write: 3 + 4 = 7. Say: *Three plus four equals seven.*

- Give pairs six red and six yellow cubes, along with Teacher Tool 5: Number Lines to 12. Write various facts to 12 and ask pairs to model them. Ensure one addend is 1, 2, or 3 so the number line can be used to count on. Have one child use cubes to show the addends while the other says the sum. Reverse the order of the addends and repeat, until everyone models the addends and finds the sum.

- Write 6 + 0. Ask: *What is the sum of these numbers?* Point out that when 0 is added to a number, the sum is always the same as the other addend. Reverse the addends. Ask: *What is the sum?* Say: *Six plus zero equals six.* Hand out Learning Resource 2 for children to complete.

Challenge Ask pairs to draw dots in two colors on an index card "domino" to show a sum to 20. They then exchange cards with another pair and write two number sentences for each domino. Collect the cards to use in the next activity.

Multilevel Strategies

1 Preproduction
Say two numbers and ask children to hold up the domino cards.

Writing Ask children to write a number sentence with the two numbers.

2 3 Early Production and Speech Emergence
Ask children to choose a domino card and use it to say a number sentence, e.g., 13 + 7 = 20.

Writing Ask children to write the number sentence. Then ask them to reverse the addends.

4 5 Intermediate and Advanced Fluency
Ask children to choose two domino cards and to say two number sentences for a partner to solve.

Writing Ask children to write about what happens when the order of addends is turned around.

Name _____

Fish for Numbers

Pick two different numbers from the fish bowl for each problem.

Write a number sentence.

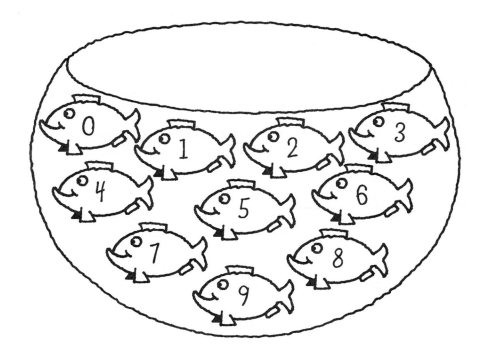

1. __5__ + __3__ = __8__   2. ____ + ____ = ____

3. ____ + ____ = ____   4. ____ + ____ = ____

5. ____ + ____ = ____   6. ____ + ____ = ____

7. ____ + ____ = ____   8. ____ + ____ = ____

 45 minutes

▶ **Key Strategy**
Use manipulatives

▶ **Format**
Whole class and student pairs

▶ **Math Vocabulary**
double(s), doubles plus one, make a ten

▶ **Daily Vocabulary**
strategy

▶ **Resources**
Learning Resource 3
Teacher Tool 4

Materials
- counters
- number cards for doubles
- number cubes

Assessment

Check children's mastery of the lesson vocabulary by observing them as they complete the lesson. See Assessment Checklist on page 27.

Home Connection

Have children take home their Learning Resource page to share with their family members. Ask children to explain to a family member different strategies they used to add three numbers.

Add Three Numbers

Math Objective	**ESL/TESOL Descriptors**
■ Add three 1-digit numbers.	■ Use context to construct meaning.
	■ Follow oral and written directions.

Activate Prior Knowledge Put a small pile of counters on a desk and count them. Add three counters and ask: *How many do I have now?* Point out that children have just used the strategy of counting on to add. Tell children that in this lesson they will learn more strategies for adding.

Hands-on Lesson Write: 7 + 3. Draw a ten-frame and model how to find the sum. Say: *Put seven counters in the frame. Count on three counters.* Hand out Teacher Tool 4: Ten-Frame and counters to pairs. Have children add facts to 10 using the ten-frame. Tell children that **making a ten** is a strategy for adding three numbers.

- Give pairs 20 counters and ask them to make two groups of five. Ask: *What do you notice about the two groups?* (They are the same; they are **doubles**.) Tell children that knowing doubles is also a strategy for adding three numbers.

- Play a doubles game with counters. Say a number between 0 and 9. Ask pairs to make two groups, find the sum, and raise their hands. Record each double.

- Next, explain the **doubles plus one** strategy. Say: *I say 3 + 3 = 6 and then I add one.* Repeat the activity above, recording each doubles plus one.

- Ask: *What are the three strategies that will help us add numbers?* (make a ten, doubles, doubles plus one) Hand out Learning Resource 3: Add Three Numbers. Discuss the examples before children complete the worksheet.

Challenge Give pairs number cubes. One child rolls three numbers; the other records the numbers. Have children work together to find the sum. Encourage them to use one of the strategies they have learned.

Multilevel Strategies

1 Preproduction
Write *make a ten, doubles,* and *doubles plus one.* Write and say 6 + 7 and ask children to point to the strategy they could use.

Writing Ask children to write the name of the strategy.

2 3 Early Production and Speech Emergence
Write 6 + 7 and ask children which strategy they could use to find the sum.

Writing Ask children to write the name of the strategy in a simple sentence.

4 5 Intermediate and Advanced Fluency
Write 6 + 7 and ask children to explain how they could use a strategy to find the sum.

Writing Ask children to write how they could use a strategy to solve the problem.

Name _____

Add Three Numbers

Draw a circle around the strategy you can use to add the numbers. The first three problems are done for you.

1.
$$3 \atop 3 \Big\rangle 6$$
$$+ \quad 2$$
$$\boxed{8}$$

(doubles)

doubles plus one

2.
$$6 \atop 4 \Big\rangle 10$$
$$+ \quad 2$$
$$\boxed{12}$$

(make a ten)

doubles

3.
$$6 \atop 6 \Big\rangle 12$$
$$+ \quad 1$$
$$\boxed{13}$$

make a ten

(doubles plus one)

4.
$$3$$
$$4$$
$$+ \quad 7$$
$$\boxed{}$$

doubles

make a 10

5.
$$9$$
$$0$$
$$+ \quad 9$$
$$\boxed{}$$

doubles

doubles plus one

6.
$$4$$
$$1$$
$$+ \quad 4$$
$$\boxed{}$$

doubles plus one

doubles

7.
$$0$$
$$9$$
$$+ \quad 1$$
$$\boxed{}$$

make a ten

doubles

8.
$$6$$
$$4$$
$$+ \quad 1$$
$$\boxed{}$$

doubles

make a ten

9.
$$8$$
$$2$$
$$+ \quad 8$$
$$\boxed{}$$

doubles plus one

doubles

Lesson 4

45 minutes

▶ **Key Strategy**
Use manipulatives

▶ **Format**
Whole class and student pairs

▶ **Math Vocabulary**
count back, difference, related facts, subtract

▶ **Daily Vocabulary**
between, draw a line

▶ **Resources**
Learning Resource 4
Teacher Tool 5
Overhead Manipulatives

Materials
• connecting cubes
• crayons
• index cards

Assessment

Check children's mastery of the lesson vocabulary by observing them as they complete the lesson. See page 27 for Assessment Checklist.

Home Connection

Have children take home their Learning Resource page. Ask children to work with a family member to write a related addition and subtraction sentence to share with the class.

Subtraction Skills

Math Objectives	**ESL/TESOL Descriptors**
■ Subtract facts to 20.	■ Use context to construct meaning.
■ Relate addition and subtraction.	■ Practice new language.

Activate Prior Knowledge Ask children to guess what you are doing as you slowly draw a number line. Ask: *What do you know about number lines?* Tell children that today they will use a number line to **subtract,** or **count back.**

Hands-on Lesson Display eight red and two yellow cubes. Ask: *How can you subtract to show the difference between these two groups?* Show how to count back two cubes to find the **difference.** Then use the number line to count back. Say: *Start with the greater number, 8, and count back 2. The difference is 6.* Write $8 - 2 = 6$.

• Give pairs Teacher Tool 5: Number Lines plus 18 red and 9 yellow connecting cubes. Write subtraction facts to 12. Ask pairs to model the differences using cubes and the number line. You may want to use Connecting Cubes from **Overhead Manipulatives.**

• Write $7 - 0$. Say: *What is the difference? When we subtract 0 from a number, the* difference *is always the same as the first number.*

• Write $7 + 5 = 12$ and $12 - 5 = 7$. Ask: *What is the same about these number sentences? (same three numbers) What is different? (one is addition, the other is subtraction)* Tell children these are **related facts.** Point out that they can use addition facts to help them subtract. Write number sentences with differences to 18, and invite pairs to solve them. Then hand out Learning Resource 4.

Challenge Write a series, such as 3, 5, 7, 9. Say: *I am doing something to each number, and that this is the rule you must guess. (add 2)* Whoever guesses the rule makes up the next series.

Multilevel Strategies

1 Preproduction
Say and write $18 - 9$ on the board. Ask children to count back on the number line and point to the difference.

Writing Ask children to write the number sentence $18 - 9$ and solve it.

2 3 Early Production and Speech Emergence
Write $18 - 9$ on the board and have children use the number line to count back and tell the difference.

Writing Ask children to write the number sentence, solve it, and write a new number sentence.

4 5 Intermediate and Advanced Fluency
Write $18 - 9$ on the board and ask children to explain how to use a number line to count back.

Writing Write $18 - 9$ and ask children to write a word problem that goes with the number sentence.

Name _____

A Matching Game!

Write the sum or difference. Then draw a line between the related facts.

1.
```
    9
+   9
─────
  [18]
```

```
  1 1
─   4
─────
  [  ]
```

2.
```
  1 5
─   8
─────
  [  ]
```

```
    6
+   6
─────
  [  ]
```

3.
```
  1 5
─   9
─────
  [  ]
```

```
  1 8
─   9
─────
  [ 9]
```

4.
```
    7
+   4
─────
  [  ]
```

```
    7
+   8
─────
  [  ]
```

5.
```
  1 2
─   6
─────
  [  ]
```

```
    9
+   6
─────
  [  ]
```

Lesson 5

 45 minutes

▶ **Key Strategy**
Use manipulatives

▶ **Format**
Whole class and student pairs

▶ **Math Vocabulary**
addend, missing addend, related fact

▶ **Daily Vocabulary**
under

▶ **Resource**
Learning Resource 5

Materials
• connecting cubes

Assessment

Check children's mastery of the lesson vocabulary by observing them as they complete the lesson. See Assessment Checklist on page 27.

Home Connection

Have children take home their Learning Resource page. Ask children to work with a family member to write number names for 9 to share with the class.

Missing Addends

Math Objectives	ESL/TESOL Descriptors
■ Relate addition and subtraction. ■ Use fact families to add and subtract.	■ Participate in full class, group, and pair discussions. ■ Use negotiation and manage interaction to accomplish tasks.

Activate Prior Knowledge Write $7 + 2 = 9$ on the board. Ask: *How can you use an addition fact to find a subtraction fact?* Ask children what they remember about related facts. Write $9 - 2 = 7$. Remind children that related facts use the same numbers. Write: $6 + 2 = 8, 5 + 4 = 9$, and $9 + 2 = 11$. Ask volunteers to write the related subtraction fact under each addition fact.

Hands-on Lesson Write $8 + \square = 11$ on the board. Ask: *How can you find the missing addend?* Elicit from children that they can rewrite the number sentence this way: $11 - 8 = \square$. Ask: *What is the difference?* Say: *The missing addend is 3.*

• Hand out 12 red and 12 yellow cubes to pairs. One child writes a missing addend fact to 12. The other child writes a related fact to find the missing addend. Encourage children to use cubes to help them solve the problems.

• Write *12* on the board. Ask: *What facts have this sum?* Encourage children to recall basic facts with sums and differences to 12. As children name the facts, have a volunteer write them. Point out there are many ways to make a number.

• Assign several numbers between 8 and 12 to student pairs. Ask them to find how many ways they can write each number. Invite a volunteer from each pair to share all the facts they recalled to make that number. Then hand out Learning Resource 5: Number Names and have children work on their own.

Challenge Write *17* on the board. Have children work in small groups to find as many ways to make the number 17 as possible. List them on the board.

Multilevel Strategies

1 Preproduction
Write *14* on the board. Name different ways to make the number and have children model them with cubes.

Writing Ask children to write different ways to make 14.

2 3 Early Production and Speech Emergence
Write *14* on the board and ask children to say as many ways as they can to make the number.

Writing Write *14* on the board and ask children to write as many ways as they can to make the number.

4 5 Intermediate and Advanced Fluency
Ask children to tell you ways to make 14 and then say related facts.

Writing Ask children to write the related facts.

Name _____

Number Names

Look at the number. Then circle ways to make the number.

1.

2.

 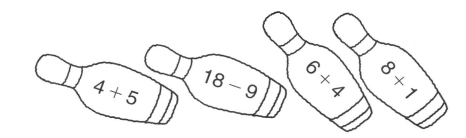

3.

 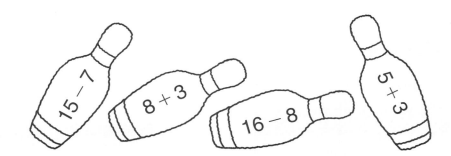

3.

Write your own ways to make 12.

▶ **Key Strategy**
Use manipulatives

▶ **Format**
Whole class and student pairs

▶ **Math Vocabulary**
fact family

▶ **Daily Vocabulary**
cube train, set of numbers

▶ **Resource**
Learning Resource 6

Materials
- counters
- cubes
- premade ten-frame

Assessment

Check children's mastery of the lesson vocabulary by observing them as they complete the lesson. See Assessment Checklist on page 27.

Home Connection

Have children take home their Learning Resource page. Ask children to work with a family member to write a fact family for 15 to share with the class.

Add and Subtract 7, 8, 9

Math Objectives	ESL/TESOL Descriptors
■ Use 10 to add and subtract 7, 8, and 9.	■ Participate in full class, group, and pair discussions.
■ Use fact families to add and subtract.	■ Use context to construct meaning.

Activate Prior Knowledge Write 6 + 4. Display a ten-frame and ten red and ten yellow counters. Ask: *How can you use the 10-frame to find the sum?* Ask a child to put six red counters in a ten-frame and count on four yellow counters. Repeat with other addition facts to 10.

Hands-on Lesson Review strategies for adding. *(make a ten, doubles, doubles plus one)* Tell children now they will learn a new strategy for adding and subtracting.

- Display a large premade ten-frame and 20 red and yellow counters. Write 9 + 5. Tell children they can make a ten to help them add larger numbers.

- Ask a child to put nine red counters in the ten-frame. Ask another child to put five yellow counters in the ten-frame to make a ten. Ask another child to put the four other counters next to the ten-frame. Encourage the child to say: *I make a ten and have four ones.* Repeat using 7, 8, and 9 to add.

- Write 15 − 7. Put ten red counters in the ten-frame and five counters next to it. Ask a child to take away seven counters. Ask: *How many are left?* Then subtract eight and nine.

- Make a cube train with six red and three blue cubes. Ask: *What set of numbers is in this cube train?* (6, 3, 9) Say: *We can use these numbers to make a fact family: 6 + 3 = 9, 3 + 6 = 9, 9 − 6 = 3, 9 − 3 = 6.* Point out a fact family for a double has only two facts. Hand out Learning Resource 6: Fact Families.

Challenge Ask pairs to write fact families for 16, 9, and 7. Ask them to describe each one, including how many numbers it has, how many addition number sentences, how many subtraction number sentences, and so on.

Multilevel Strategies

❶ Preproduction
Write 9 + 7 on the board and ask children to model it using a ten-frame and counters.

Writing Ask children to write the name of one strategy they have learned to add and subtract numbers.

❷❸ Early Production and Speech Emergence
Ask children to model 9 + 7 using a ten-frame and counters, using simple sentences.

Writing Ask children to write the names of two strategies for adding and subtracting numbers.

❹❺ Intermediate and Advanced Fluency
Ask children to explain how to model 9 + 7 using a ten-frame and counters.

Writing Ask children to write the names of the strategies they have learned for adding and subtracting numbers.

Name _____

Fact Families

Complete each fact family.

1.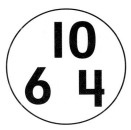

$6 + 4 = \underline{10}$ $10 - 6 = \underline{4}$

$4 + 6 = \underline{10}$ $10 - 4 = \underline{6}$

2.

$6 + 6 = \underline{12}$ $12 - 6 = \underline{6}$

3.

$9 + 6 = \underline{}$ $15 - 9 = \underline{}$

$6 + 9 = \underline{}$ $15 - 6 = \underline{}$

Now try writing fact families yourself.

4.

_____   _____

_____   _____

5.

_____   _____

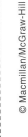

© Macmillan/McGraw-Hill

Problem Solving
Reading for Math

SKILL: Important and Unimportant Information
Model the skill using a word problem such as the following:

① I'm going to the library tomorrow. I'm going to take out 3 mystery books. I'll take out 2 books on reptiles, too. Reptiles have scales on their bodies. How many books will I take out in all?

② I can count on to find the number of books I will take out.

③ **Think:** How many mystery books will I take out?
I'll take out 3 mystery books.
Think: How many books on reptiles will I take out?
I'll take out 2 books on reptiles.
Think: How many books will I take out in all?
I'll count on 2 starting from 3. I'll take out 5 books in all.

④ What was the **important information?**
I needed to know how many mystery books and how many books on reptiles I want to take out.
What was the **unimportant information?**
I didn't need to know that reptiles are covered with scales.

Distribute **Math Center Card 1A** to children.

Math Center Card 1A

Reading for Math Skill

IMPORTANT AND UNIMPORTANT INFORMATION • PLAN A PARTY

1. Read the story problem to your partner. Tell your partner to listen carefully to all the information.

2. Work together to solve the problem.

> We need lots of balloons at the party. You get 49 blue balloons. Get some big balloons. I will get 23 red balloons.
>
> Red is my favorite color. How many balloons will we have?

3. Circle the important information. Cross out the unimportant information.

Math Center Card, Grade 2, Unit 1, 1A

STRATEGY: Draw a Picture
Model the strategy using a word problem such as the following:

Read Vera took the training wheels off her bicycle. Now her bike has 2 wheels. Her little brother rides a tricycle. How many wheels do they have in all?

Plan I can draw a picture. First I'll draw a picture of Vera's bicycle. Then I'll draw a picture of her brother's tricycle. Then I can count the wheels.

Solve I can carry out my plan. There are 2 wheels on Vera's bicycle. The tricycle has 3 wheels. I count 5 wheels in all. 2 + 3 = 5.

Look Back I'll check my answer again. This time I'll count on 3 starting from 2. There are five wheels in all.
Does my answer make sense? Yes.

Distribute **Math Center Card 1B** to children.

Math Center Card 1B

Problem Solving: Strategy

DRAW A PICTURE • HOW MANY APPLES?

You need: crayons, paper

1. Read the story with a partner. Work together to answer the questions.

Jack and Mark picked some apples. Jack picked 6 apples. Mark picked 5 apples. How many apples did they pick altogether?

2. What do you need to find?

3. Draw a picture to help you solve the problem. Use a red crayon to show how many apples Jack picked. Use a green crayon to show how many apples Mark picked.

4. Now write a number sentence that shows how many apples in all. What is the answer?

5. Check your answer. Count all the apples in your picture. Does the number match your answer?

Math Center Card, Grade 2, Unit 1, 1B

Assessment Checklist

	STUDENT NAMES										
SCHOOL:											
TEACHER: **SCHOOL YEAR:**											
Mark: + = Mastery √ = Satisfactory − = Needs Improvement											
LEVEL OF LANGUAGE PROFICIENCY (1–5)											
MATH OBJECTIVES											
• Add three 1-digit numbers.											
• Add and subtract, facts to 20.											
• Identify number patterns.											
• Relate addition and subtraction.											
• Use fact families to add and subtract.											
ESL/TESOL LISTENING/SPEAKING											
Focus attention selectively.											
Follow oral and written directions.											
Listen to and imitate how others use English.											
Participate in full class, group, and pair discussions.											
Use negotiation and manage interaction to accomplish tasks.											
ESL/TESOL READING											
Read about subject matter information.											
Apply basic reading comprehension skills.											
Follow written directions, implicit and explicit.											
ESL WRITING											
Write to demonstrate comprehension.											
Write using spelling patterns and targeted English vocabulary.											

Foldables

❶ Preproduction
- Did children write the unit vocabulary?
- Did they write the vocabulary words?
- Did they copy the definitions?

❷ ❸ Early Production and Speech Emergence
- Did children label the tabs correctly?

❹ ❺ Intermediate and Advanced Fluency
- Did children write definitions for the unit vocabulary?
- Did they use correct spelling and grammar?

Exploring Number Relationships

Numbers

Number Problems

Understand Addition and Subtraction

Number	Subtract All		Number	Subtract Zero		Number	Count back to Subtract

 # Planner
Place Value and Money

Assessment
p. 49
• Assessment Checklist
• Foldables

LOG ON Visit **www.mmhmath.com**

Unit Activities	
• **Activity 1** Readiness Pick a Number, p. 32	• **Activity 3** Make 100 cents or More, p. 33
• **Activity 2** I Have Enough Money, p. 32	• **Activity 4** How Many Tens and Ones?, p.33

Lessons	Key Objectives	Vocabulary	Materials	Resources
READ TOGETHER "The Difference," pp. 30–31	**Math:** Identify coins and their values. **ESL/TESOL:** Goal 1, Standard 1.	between, cent, difference, dime, exactly, penny, question, value		
UNIT WARM-UP Understanding Numbers to 100 p. 34	**Math:** Count, read, write, and represent numbers to 100. **ESL/TESOL:** Goal 1, Standard 3.	ones, tens	base ten materials, beans	**Overhead Manipulatives**
LESSON 1 Place Value pp. 36–37	**Math:** Identify the place value for each digit for numbers to 100. **ESL/TESOL:** Goal 2, Standards 1, 3.	digit, place value	beans, connecting cubes	Learning Resource 7 Teacher Tools, 1 and 3
LESSON 2 Compare and Order Numbers pp. 38–39	**Math:** Compare and order numbers to 100. Identify ordinal numbers. **ESL/TESOL:** Goal 1/2, Standards 3/2.	compare, equal to (=), greater than (>), less than (<), ordinal numbers	connecting cubes, cards: number, ordinal, symbol	Learning Resource 8
LESSON 3 Skip-Counting Patterns pp. 40–41	**Math:** Skip-count to 100. Identify odd and even numbers. **ESL/TESOL:** Goal 1/2, Standards 1/2.	after, before, between, even, number line, odd, skip–count	butcher paper, cubes, counters, glue, number cards, magazines	Learning Resource 9 **Math Rhymes CD**
LESSON 4 Estimating and Comparing Numbers pp. 42–43	**Math:** Estimate and compare numbers. **ESL/TESOL:** Goal 2, Standard 2.	estimate	counters, index cards, pipe cleaners, clear plastic cups	Learning Resource 10
LESSON 5 All Kinds of Coins pp. 44–45	**Math:** Identify coins and their values. **ESL/TESOL:** Goal 2/2, Standards 1/3.	dime (10¢), half-dollar (50¢), nickel (5¢), penny (1¢), quarter (25¢)	jar, chart paper, coins, glue, magazines, paper bags, scissors	Learning Resource 11
LESSON 6 Dollars and Cents pp. 46–47	**Math:** Identify a dollar and its value. Make change. **ESL/TESOL:** Goal 1/2, Standards 1/2.	cent sign (¢), decimal point, dollar, dollar sign ($)	coins, dollar, bills, envelope, scissors, string	Learning Resource 12 Teacher Tool 13
PROBLEM SOLVING p. 48 • Skill: Cause and Effect • Strategy: Act It Out	Use skills and strategies to solve problems.			**Math Center Cards 2A, 2B**

Planner

See **Math at Home Family Guide** for additional math vocabulary, activities, and games in English, Spanish, and Haitian Creole.

English Vocabulary

Dear Family: Please help your child practice the key vocabulary words for this unit.

cent sign (¢) the sign used to show cents

decimal point (.) separates dollars from cents

even every number that ends with 0, 2, 4, 6, or 8

odd every number that ends with 1, 3, 5, 7, or 9

ordinal number tells position

place value The value a digit has in a number. The first digit on the right is in the ones place, the second digit is in the tens place, the third digit is in the hundreds place, and so on.

Vocabulario en español

Estimados familiares: Por favor ayuden a su hijo/a a practicar las palabras del vocabulario de esta unidad.

signo de centavos (¢) signo que se usa para mostrar centavos

punto decimal (.) separa los dólares de los centavos

par cualquier número que termina en 0, 2, 4, 6 u 8

impar cualquier número que termina en 1, 3, 5, 7 ó 9

número ordinal número que indica posición

valor de posición el valor que tiene un dígito en un número; el primer dígito de la derecha está en el lugar de las unidades, el segundo está en el de las decenas, el tercero está en el de las centenas y así sucesivamente.

Vokabilè an kreyol

Chè paran: Tanpri ede pitit la pratike mo vokabilè nan seksyon sa a.

senbol santim sign ou itilize pou montre santim

pwen desimal (.) separe dola ak santim

chif pè chak nonm ki fini ak 0, 2,4,6, osnon 8

chif enpè tout nonm ki fini ak 1,3,5,7 osnon 9

nonm odinal di lod ak ran

enpotans pozisyon chif yo volè pozisyon chif yo bayo nan yon nonb. Pwemye a dwat la nan inite, dezyèm nan nan dizèn, twazyem nan nan santèn

The Difference

 30 minutes

Math Objective
- Identify coins and their values.

ESL/TESOL Descriptors
- Share and request information.
- Engage in conversations.

Reading Skill
- Make inferences

Vocabulary
between, cent, difference, dime, exactly, penny, question, value

Before Reading

Build Background/Oral Language
Hold up a penny and a dime and ask if anybody knows the names of the coins. Name the coins and ask which is larger. Say the value of each. Tell children that you will read a poem about a penny and a dime.

During Reading

- As you read, change your voice for the teacher and Dennis and hold up a penny and a dime.

- Ask: *What is the difference between a penny and a dime?* Then in the poem read: *This is the difference. Exactly nine cents.* Remind children that *difference* has two meanings.

- Reread the poem. After reading the teacher's part, pause and ask: *What can Dennis say to answer the question?* Then read the answer.

- Have one group of children read the teacher's part and the other read Dennis' response.

Phonological/Phonemic Awareness
Ask children to find words in the poem that begin with *d*: *difference, dear, Dennis,* and *dime*. Write the words. Ask children to suggest other words that begin with *d*.

After Reading

Ask pairs to make a two-column chart. Give them a dime and 10 pennies. Ask them to make rubbings of the coins on the chart. Ask: *What is the difference in how the coins look? What is the difference if you subtract one penny?*

Drama Invite children to act out the poem with a nickel and a dime. Have them use their own name instead of Dennis.

Assessment

Observe children's participation in each of the groups. See Assessment Checklist on page 49.

Multilevel Strategies

1 **Preproduction**
Write the words *penny, dime, difference* on cards for children to match to words in the poem. Say: *Find the word (penny).*

Writing Have children underline the three words above in the poem and then write the three words.

2 **3** **Early Production and Speech Emergence**
Ask: *Which is larger, a penny or a dime? What does Dennis say is the difference?*

Writing Have children write the answers to the questions above by copying them from the poem page.

4 **5** **Intermediate and Advanced Fluency**
Ask: *What does the word difference mean?* Encourage a discussion about the different meanings that words can have.

Writing Ask children to write two sentences to show the two meanings of *difference;* for example, size, subtraction.

The Difference

What is the difference between a penny and a dime? In this poem Dennis has subtraction on his mind.

What is the difference,
Dear Dennis,
Dear Dennis,
Between a penny and a dime?

This is the difference,
Dear Teacher,
Dear Teacher,
Exactly nine cents every time!

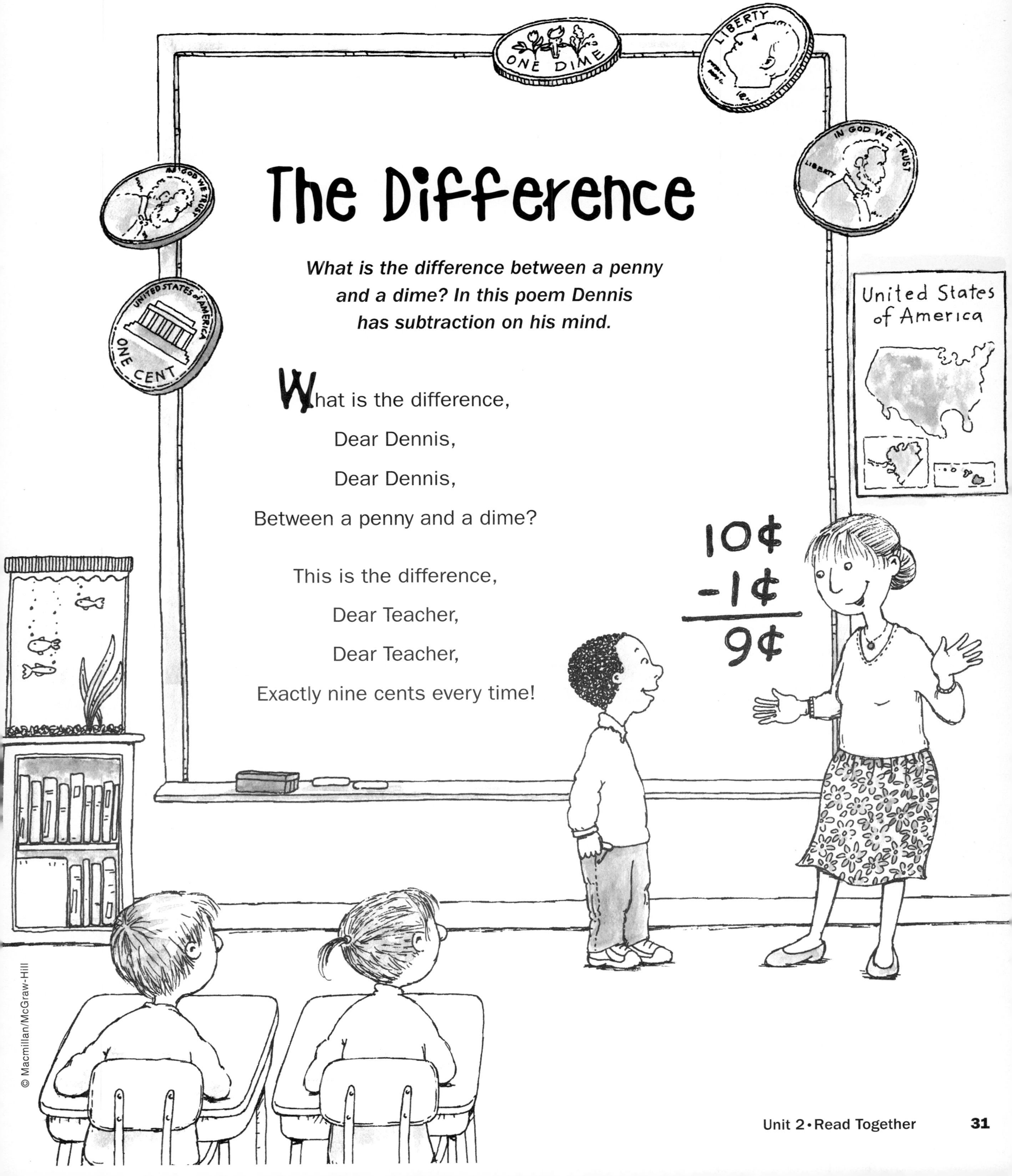
ONE DIME
LIBERTY
IN GOD WE TRUST
LIBERTY
IN GOD WE TRUST
UNITED STATES of AMERICA
ONE CENT
United States of America
10¢
-1¢
9¢

Activities

ACTIVITY 1

PARTNERS

Pick a Number

Take turns.

YOU NEED

bag

- Take 3 handfuls of cubes out of a bag.
  Organize the cubes in sets of tens.

- Write how many tens and
  ones you have.
  Write the number.

- Who has more cubes?

Play four games.

2 tens 3 ones

23

Identify Place Value

ACTIVITY 2

INDIVIDUAL

Do I Have Enough Money?

- Find 3 ads for foods that cost less than
  99 cents each.

- Cut out pictures and paste them on paper.

- You have 75 cents to spend.
  Compare 75 cents and the cost of 1 food item.
  Can you buy the food?
  Circle the food if you can buy it.

- Can you buy the other foods?
  Compare to find out.

YOU NEED

newspaper food ads
scissors
glue

BEANS 39¢

89¢ MILK

75¢ > 39¢   75¢ < 89¢

Use < for is less than
Use > for is more than

Compare Numbers to 100

Game Zone

ACTIVITY 3

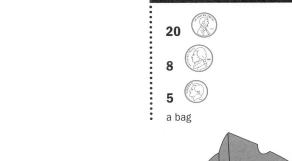
PARTNERS

Grab Bag

Take turns.

- Take some coins from the bag.
  Sort the dimes, nickels, and pennies.

- Write how much money you have.
  Your partner checks your total.
  Put the coins back in the bag.

Each of you plays 4 times.
Check your partner's work.

YOU NEED

20

8

5

a bag

39¢

Add Money Amounts

ACTIVITY 4

INDIVIDUAL

How Many Tens and Ones?

- Use the beans in Bag 1 to make counters for 10.
  Glue 10 beans to each craft stick.
  Make as many bean-stick counters as you can.

- Count and write the number of tens and ones.

- Write the number.

- Do the same for the other bags.

YOU NEED

3–4 bags of beans

craft sticks

glue (or tape)

3 tens 2 ones
32

Count Numbers to 100

© Macmillan/McGraw-Hill

Understanding Numbers to 100

25 minutes

▶ **Key Strategy**
Use manipulatives

▶ **Format**
Whole class and student pairs

▶ **Math Vocabulary**
ones, tens

▶ **Daily Vocabulary**
groups, trading

Resources
Overhead Manipulatives:
Base-Ten Models

▶ **Materials**
Base-Ten materials, beans

Math Objective	**ESL/TESOL Descriptor**
■ Count, read, write, and represent numbers to 100.	■ Use context to construct meaning.

Activate Prior Knowledge Show children 20 loose connecting cubes and say: *There are 20 cubes.* Then show two connected sets of ten cubes. Say: *There are 20 cubes here, too.* Point to the loose cubes and the groups of ten and ask: *Which is easier to count?* Elicit that it is easier to count items when they are in groups of ten. Use the words *tens* and *ones* to refer to the groups. Point out that there are 10 ones in a ten.

Hands-on Lesson Give children Base-Ten materials. Ask them to begin with a one, and then add ones until they have enough to trade for a ten. Continue to 100. Show them how to record their trades to make a list. (10 ones = 1 ten, 20 ones = 2 tens, and so on) You may wish to use the **Overhead Manipulatives:** Base-Ten Models.

● Provide pairs of children with beans. One child in each pair says a number, which the other child counts out in beans.

● After counting out the given number, ask the children to group the beans into groups of ten. Give an example: *17 would be one group of ten with seven ones left over.*

● Invite a volunteer from each pair to tell how many groups of ten there are in the number. Then ask the child how many ones are left. Ask children to write the number.

Multilevel Strategies

1 Preproduction
Ask children to use beans to model numbers that you say.

2 3 Early Production and Speech Emergence
Model a number for children using beans and ask: *What is the number?*

4 5 Intermediate and Advanced Fluency
Have children model numbers for a partner using beans. The partner should name the number and say how many groups of tens are in it and how many ones are left over.

LOG
ON
Visit **www.mmhmath.com** to find printable **Vocabulary Cards** that help build academic language.

Procedure: Help children make these Foldables to write vocabulary words and definitions throughout the unit. Encourage children to use the Foldables as a study guide.

Layered-Look Book

1. Provide each child with two sheets of 11" × 17" paper, or use two 6-foot-long sheets of bulletin board paper to make one large classroom Layered-Look Book.

2. Place the two sheets of paper an equal distance apart.

3. Roll the bottom of the two sheets up to make three tabs the same size. Fold, staple, and label the tabs as shown.

4. Have children include words, symbols, and examples of problems under the tabs.

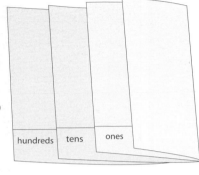

5. Children may also want to create another Layered-Look Book to practice estimating numbers or making predictions.

Going Further Children can use their Layered-Look Book to review place value by comparing their pictures and examples of hundreds, tens, and ones.

Accordion Book

1. Provide each child with three sheets of 11" × 17" paper.

2. Fold the three sheets of paper in half like a hamburger. Tape their edges together to form a 6-second study guide.

3. This can be made without using tape by folding the three sheets in half, leaving one side 1" longer than the other.

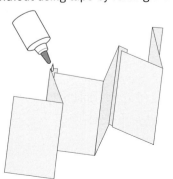

4. Fold the 1" forward over the short side, and then fold it back the other way.

5. Glue the straight edge of each sheet onto the tab of another.

6. As children work through the chapter, they can record math words, concepts, and examples of numbers and patterns under the tabs.

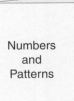

Numbers and Patterns

Going Further Children can use their Accordion Book to review the chapter by comparing their pictures and examples of numbers and number patterns.

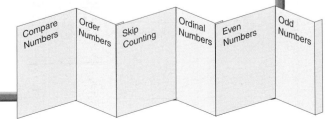

45 minutes

▶ **Key Strategy**
Use visuals

▶ **Format**
Whole class and student pairs

▶ **Math Vocabulary**
digit, place value

▶ **Daily Vocabulary**
groups, sets

▶ **Resources**
Learning Resource 7
Teacher Tools 1 and 3

Materials
• beans
• 48 connecting cubes

Assessment

Check children's mastery of place value in 2-digit numbers by observing them as they complete the lesson. See Assessment Checklist on page 49.
Remind children to work on their Foldables.

Home Connection

Have children find items at home that they can group, such as beans. Use quantities greater than 40. Encourage them to take big handfuls and then count by grouping tens and ones.

Place Value

Math Objectives	**ESL/TESOL Descriptors**
■ Identify the place value for each digit for numbers to 100.	■ Engage in conversations.
■ Count, read, write, and represent numbers to 100.	■ Practice new language.

Activate Prior Knowledge Put a pile of 48 individual connecting cubes on a table and say: *How can I group the cubes to count them?* Elicit that it is easier to connect the cubes in groups of ten to count them. Then have volunteers connect the cubes to make groups of tens and ones and count them.

Hands-on Lesson Write the number 48. Point to the 4 and then the 8. Say: *There are two digits in the number 48.* Point to the 4 and say: The digit in this place tells how many tens. There are 4 tens. Next point to the 8 and say: *The digit in this place tells how many ones.* Hold up the 4 tens and the 8 ones.

● Write 2-digit numbers and ask children to point to the digits that show the tens and the ones. Ask them to show the number by grouping connecting cubes into sets of tens and ones. Ask: *How many groups of tens are there? How many ones are there?* Help them to find the value of each place.

● Have children take turns holding up number cards, Teacher Tools 1 and 3. Ask volunteers to say the number and tell which digit is in the tens place and which is in the ones place.

● Distribute Learning Resource 7. Have children in pairs take turns choosing numbers between 10 and 99. The partner writes the number and then draws blue squares for groups of ten and yellow squares for ones.

Challenge Partners roll a number cube two times each. They write 2-digit numbers. The partner with more tens wins 5 points; if the tens are the same they look at the ones. The first to reach 50 points wins.

Multilevel Strategies

1 **Preproduction**
Say and write numbers.
Say: *Show the tens and ones in those numbers with connecting cubes.*

Writing Say a number. Have children write it using blue for the tens place and green for the ones place.

2 3 **Early Production and Speech Emergence**
Show 2-digit numbers.
Ask: *How many tens are there? How many ones?*

Writing Say a 2-digit number (56). Ask children to write how many tens and ones it has.

4 5 **Intermediate and Advanced Fluency**
Have children describe a number. For example, *The 9 is in the tens place. The 6 is in the ones place. There are 9 tens and 6 ones.*

Writing Ask children to write the description of the number.

Name _____

Draw Tens and Ones

Write a 2-digit number. Draw squares to show how many tens and how many ones are in the number. Draw one blue square for each ten and one yellow square for each one.

NUMBER	TENS	ONES

Lesson 2

 45 minutes

▶ **Key Strategy**
Use manipulatives

▶ **Format**
Whole class and student pairs

▶ **Math Vocabulary**
compare, is equal to (=), is greater than (>), is less than (<), ordinal numbers (first to tenth)

▶ **Daily Vocabulary**
fewer, less, more, position, symbol, total, value

▶ **Resource**
Learning Resource 8

Materials
• connecting cubes
• number cards 1–100
• ordinal number cards
• symbol cards
 (< , > , =)

Compare and Order Numbers

Math Objectives	**ESL/TESOL Descriptors**
■ Compare and order numbers to 100.	■ Compare and contrast information.
■ Identify ordinal numbers.	■ Use context to construct meaning.

Activate Prior Knowledge Ask two children to take big handfuls of cubes, and make trains of ten. Ask: *How many cubes do you have?* Ask: *Who has more cubes? Who has fewer cubes?* Point out that to compare numbers they first look at the tens and then the ones.

Hands-on Lesson Write **is less than** <, **is greater than** >, and **is equal to** = on the board. Write *56* and *72* and work with the class to compare. Ask: *What is the value of the ten in each number?* Write: *56 is less than 72.* Underneath it write *56 < 72.* Do the same to practice is greater than and is equal to.

• Hand out symbol cards and buckets of connecting cubes to pairs. Each player takes two handfuls of cubes from the bucket and makes trains of ten. He or she says the number and whether it is greater or is less than another number. For example, *47 is less than 49; 49 is greater than 47.* Have players make number sentences using cards. For example, **47 < 49; 49 < 47.**

• Write the ordinal number words **first** through **tenth** and 1st–10th. Point out that they can be written in words only or in numbers and letters (1st has the letters *st* from *first*, etc.). Get in a line with children and say: *I'm first. Lee is second.* Repeat your place and ask children to name their places.

• Hand out Learning Resource 8 and have children complete the page in pairs.

Challenge Divide children into small groups and give each group number cards 1–100. Have children shuffle the cards and work together to put them in order.

Multilevel Strategies

1 Preproduction
Hold up the word cards *first, second,* and *third.* Say each word and ask children to hold up the matching number card.

Writing Hold up ordinal word cards (*first, second, etc*) and have children write the numbers.

2 3 Early Production and Speech Emergence
Hold up cards from first to tenth as you say each word. Ask children to repeat the word and hold up the matching number.

Writing Hold up number cards *1st–10th* and have children write the word.

4 5 Intermediate and Advanced Fluency
Hand out ordinal number cards. Take turns putting the cards in order while the group says the numbers.

Writing Encourage children to write a phrase or sentence using an ordinal number.

8

Name _____

Number Parade

Look at the animals' signs. Circle the animal's place in the parade.

1. first fourth	**2.** seventh tenth
3. third fifth	**4.** sixth eighth

Write the numbers.

tenth _____   ninth _____

eighth _____   fourth _____

second _____   seventh _____

first _____   fifth _____

third _____   sixth _____

 45 minutes

▶ **Key Strategy**
Use visuals

▶ **Format**
Whole class and student pairs

▶ **Math Vocabulary**
after, before, between, even, number line, odd, skip-count

▶ **Daily Vocabulary**
easier, fast, group (noun and verb)

▶ **Resources**
Learning Resource 9
Math Rhymes CD:
"2, 4, 6, 8!"

Materials
- connecting cubes
- counters
- number cards
- old magazines

Assessment

Observe children's use of the vocabulary as they complete the lesson. See Assessment Checklist on page 49.
Remind children to work on thewir Foldables.

Home Connection

Family members can take a handful of beans and guess whether the total is even or odd. Together they can skip-count by twos, fives, or tens to find the total.

Skip-Counting Patterns

Math Objectives	ESL/TESOL Descriptors
■ Skip-count to 100. ■ Identify odd and even numbers.	■ Select, connect, and explain information. ■ Follow oral and written directions, implicit and explicit.

Activate Prior Knowledge Play "2, 4, 6, 8!" from the **Math Rhymes CD**. Hand out bags of 50 counters. Ask pairs to make groups of two counters and count them. Then have them make groups of fives and tens and count.

Hands-on Lesson Draw a **number line** with 0–50. Ask: *How do you* **skip-count** *to 10 by twos?* Draw "skips" of two spaces, from 0–10. Write the numbers beneath the line. Have volunteers draw skips for 10–50.

● Write a number pattern, such as 50, 52, 54, and ask: *What number comes* **before** *54? What comes* **between** *50 and 54? What comes* **after** *54?* Make a line and ask children to count off one by one. Ask the children to line up in pairs, and have them count off by twos.

● Write a number and **even** and **odd**. Ask: *Is this number even or odd?* Point out that even numbers can be made with pairs and odd numbers cannot. If the last digit is 0, 2, 4, 6, or 8, the number is even. If it is 3, 5, 7, or 9, the number is odd. Distribute number cards to pairs. One child flips the top card over. The first child to touch the card and call out "even" or "odd" wins the card. Have each player count how many cards they won and tell if the number is even or odd.

● Distribute Learning Resource 9: Dot Pairs. When children have completed it, invite them to create a skip-counting problem of their own.

Challenge Make a collage in four sections. Write four questions: *What comes in. . . (twos, fours, even numbers, odd numbers)?* Children paste magazine pictures, such as a dog with four legs, or the eyes on a face.

Multilevel Strategies

❶ Preproduction
Ask children to use connecting cubes to model even and odd numbers between 1–20 that you say and write on the board.

Writing Have children copy from the board each number they model.

❷❸ Early Production and Speech Emergence
Say "even" or "odd." Invite a volunteer to name an appropriate number.

Writing Have children list the even and odd numbers in two columns.

❹❺ Intermediate and Advanced Fluency
Ask children to explain how they know whether a number is even or odd.

Writing Have children write sentences that tell the difference between even and odd numbers.

Name _____

Dot Pairs

Circle pairs of dots. Write the number.

Circle whether the number is even or odd.

1. ● ● ● ● ● ● ● ● ● ● ●
   ● ● ● ● ● ● ● ● ● ● ●   _____

                                            even   odd

2. ● ● ● ● ● ● ● ● ●   _____

                                            even   odd

3. ● ● ● ● ● ● ● ● ●
   ● ● ● ● ● ● ●   _____

                                            even   odd

4. ● ● ● ● ● ● ● ● ● ● ●
   ● ● ● ● ● ● ● ● ● ● ● ●   _____

                                            even   odd

⏱ **45 minutes**

▶ **Key Strategy**
Use visuals

▶ **Format**
Whole class and student pairs

▶ **Math Vocabulary**
estimate

▶ **Daily Vocabulary**
about how many, close, count, exact, less than, more than, reasonable

▶ **Resource**
Learning Resource 10

Materials
- clear plastic cups
- counters
- index cards
- pipe cleaners

Assessment

Check children's mastery of the lesson vocabulary by observing them as they complete the lesson. See Assessment Checklist on page 49.

Home Connection

Have children take home the Learning Resource page to show their family. They can work with a family member to draw a new problem on the back of the page to share with classmates.

Estimating and Comparing

Math Objectives	ESL/TESOL Descriptors
■ Estimate numbers.	■ Hypothesize and predict.
■ Compare numbers.	■ Demonstrate knowledge through application in a variety of contexts.

Activate Prior Knowledge Put five counters in your hand and ask: *How many counters do I have?* Walk around and let children count them. Then show a box or jar filled with counters. Ask: *How many counters do I have now?* Point out that the number is too large to count easily. We make an **estimate,** or a reasonable guess to say *about how many* there are.

Hands-on Lesson

- Distribute pipe cleaners and a clear plastic cup to each group. Fill a cup with pipe cleaners and show it to children. Have children count five pipe cleaners into their cup. Invite them to compare it to the demonstration cup. Ask children to use their cup as a guide to estimate the number of pipe cleaners that are in the first cup. Have each group write down their estimate on an index card.

- Ask groups to hold up their estimates. Compare the estimates as a class, and then ask a volunteer to count the pipe cleaners in the demonstration cup by groups of five so children can see how close their estimates were.

- Distribute Learning Resource 10: Stars in a Jar and have children work in pairs.

Challenge Fill a jar with about 75 pipe cleaners. Ask children to estimate if the number of pipe cleaners is greater than or less than 100. Take a vote. After children have voted, ask them to explain how they made their estimate.

Multilevel Strategies

1 Preproduction
Place a large handful of counters and a group of ten counters on a table. Write numbers and ask children to point to the one that is a reasonable estimate.

Writing Have children write their estimates on index cards.

2 3 Early Production and Speech Emergence
Place counters on a table. Group ten. Ask children to estimate the number, and count to compare.

Writing Have children write if their estimate is greater than, less than, or equal to the total number.

4 5 Intermediate and Advanced Fluency
Place counters on a table. Group ten. Have children estimate the total and say how the group of ten helped them.

Writing Ask them to write how they made an estimate.

Name _____

Stars in a Jar

Look at each box below. Draw a ring around ten stars. Then draw a circle around the number that you think is the most reasonable estimate.

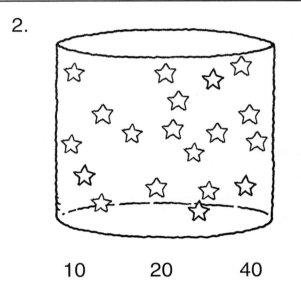

1.

20   30   50

2.

10   20   40

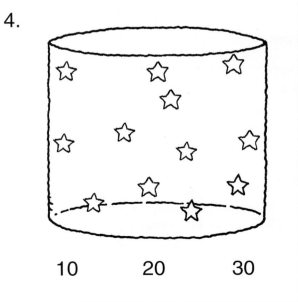

3.

20   30   40

4.

10   20   30

Lesson 5

 45 minutes

▶ **Key Strategy**
Use realia

▶ **Format**
Whole class, small groups

▶ **Math Vocabulary**
dime (10¢), half–dollar
(50¢), nickel (5¢), penny
(1¢), quarter (25¢)

▶ **Daily Vocabulary**
coin, color, gold, greatest,
least, money, value, silver,
size, worth

▶ **Resource**
Learning Resource 11

Materials
• clear jar or piggy bank
• coins (pennies, nickels,
  dimes, quarters, half–
  dollars)
• magazines and flyers
• paper bags

Assessment

Check children's use of vocabulary
as they complete the lesson. See
Assessment Checklist on page 49.
Remind children to work on their
Foldables.

Home Connection

Invite children to take home
Learning Resource 11. Ask a
family member to put a handful
of coins on a table to draw and
count. Children can share their
drawings with the class.

All Kinds of Coins

Math Objectives	**ESL/TESOL Descriptors**
■ Identify coins and their values. ■ Find the value of a set of coins.	■ Use context to construct meaning. ■ Negotiate and manage information to accomplish tasks.

Activate Prior Knowledge Display a jar or piggy bank filled with different
coins. Ask children to name all the coin words they know. Write them on chart
paper. Hold up each of the coins and talk about their colors and size.

Hands-on Lesson Ask children to help you make a Money Word Wall that
includes the name of each coin and its value.

• Model sorting and counting coins by value. Display four **dimes**, two **nickels** and
  three **pennies.** Show how we can skip count to find the total value of the coins.

• Give bags of pennies, nickels, and dimes to small groups. Make sure total
  amounts are under $1.00 and that groups have different totals. Ask children to
  arrange their coins in rows from greatest to least.

• Have groups look at the row of coins they have made. Ask: *What is a fast way to
  count your row of coins?* (skip-count). Say: *Skip-count by tens and fives and then
  count on by ones to find the total value of the coins*.

• Ask a volunteer from each group to write the total value of the coins on the
  board. Point to two totals, and have children compare the money amounts using
  these phrases: *is less than, is greater than,* and *is equal to.*

• Add quarters and half–dollars, and repeat the activity above.

• Distribute Learning Resource 11 and ask pairs to complete the page.

Cultural Link Invite children to bring in coins from their native countries and
show them to the rest of the class.

Multilevel Strategies

① Preproduction
Display coins, and give
directions such as: **Point
to a penny. Point to a coin
that is 25 cents. Pick up
a dime. Use two coins to
show 15 cents.**

Writing Have children
copy a list of the names of
coins and their values.

**② ③ Early Production
and Speech Emergence**
Ask children to say the
name and value of each
coin as you show it.

Writing Have children
write the name of each
coin that you hold up.

**④ ⑤ Intermediate
and Advanced Fluency**
Give out coins to each child
and have them tell what
they have in full sentences.

Writing Use bags of coins
and have children write
directions for a classmate
to follow. For example,
"take out two quarters."

Name _____

Buy a Keychain Charm

Show two ways you can buy the charm. In each box, draw a circle around the coins you need.

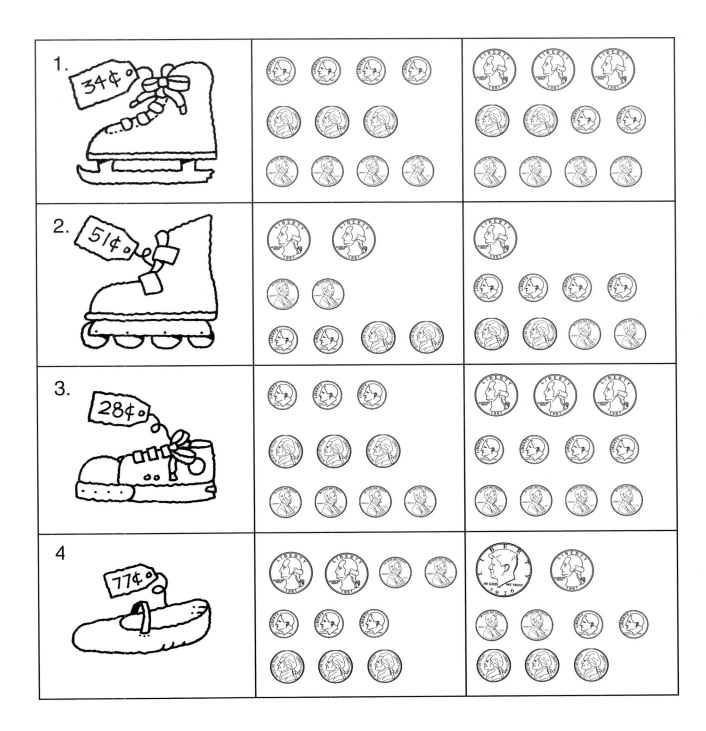

Lesson 6

 45 minutes

▶ **Key Strategy**
Use visuals

▶ **Format**
Small groups and student pairs

▶ **Math Vocabulary**
cent sign (¢), decimal point, dollar, dollar sign ($)

▶ **Daily Vocabulary**
clerk, coin, compare, cost, make change, money, pet, price, store, value

▶ **Resources**
Learning Resource 12
Teacher Tool 13

Materials
- coins and dollar bills
- envelope
- string

Assessment

Check children's mastery of the lesson vocabulary as they complete the lesson. See Assessment Checklist on page 49. Remind children to work on their Foldables.

Home Connection

Ask children to find a sale item between $1.00 and $2.00 in a flyer, cut it out, and paste it on paper. Invite children to practice purchasing and making change with a family member.

Dollars and Cents

Math Objectives	**ESL/TESOL Descriptors**
■ Identify a dollar and its value.	■ Conduct transactions.
■ Make change.	■ Represent information visually and interpret information presented visually.

Activate Prior Knowledge Hold up coins and ask children to say their names and values. Then show a **dollar** bill and ask what it is called. Ask if anyone knows the value of a dollar. Write the number 100 and the value 100¢ and $1.00. Ask a child to point to what is different in each one. Discuss the **dollar sign,** the **cent sign,** and the **decimal point.** Add these terms to a Money Word Wall.

Hands-on Lesson Group children. Hand out envelopes of different coin combinations from Teacher Tool 13 that equal between $1.00 and $2.00. Ask children to find two ways to make $1.00. Tell children they are going to set up a classroom pet store. Brainstorm a list of animals they would find in a pet store.

- Ask pairs to draw and cut out an animal on the list. Have them write a price less than $2.00 on a price tag made of tagboard and attach it with string. Post a pet store sign, and ask each pair to display their animal and its price in the pet store.

- Model a transaction at the pet store. Invite a volunteer to be the clerk. Ask: **How much is the (dog)?** Open your wallet (envelope), and invite children to help count your money. Ask if you have enough (If you do not, move on to another animal). Pay the clerk more than the cost. Then ask: **What will the clerk do now?** (make change) Model for children how to make change by counting on from the price of the animal, starting with pennies and then nickels and dimes.

- Hand out money envelopes to pairs and let them take turns being the customer and the clerk. Then hand Learning Resource 12 and have them complete it.

Challenge Have children choose an animal from the pet store, write its price and draw two different combinations of coins to show the price.

Multilevel Strategies

1 **Preproduction**
Name prices of animals in the pet store and ask children to point to the animal with that price.

Writing Have children write the name and price of their favorite pet at the store.

2 **3** **Early Production and Speech Emergence**
Ask children to name different animals from the pet store and say how much they cost.

Writing Ask children to make a list of the animals and their prices.

4 **5** **Intermediate and Advanced Fluency**
Ask children to create riddles about the animals in the store including their price.

Writing Have children write the riddles and answers.

Name _____

Counting Coins

1. Count on by .

$ ___ . ____

2. Count on by .

$ ___ . ____

3. Count on by .

$ ___ . ____

4. Count on by .

$ ___ . ____

5. What are the fewest number of coins you can use to show 50¢? Draw the coins.

6. Show $1.25 in two ways. Draw and label money amounts.

Problem Solving
Reading for Math

SKILL: Cause and Effect

Model the skill using a word problem such as the following:

1 You want to buy a big balloon. It costs 75¢. Your mom will give you 1 quarter if you help fold the clothes. Your dad will give you 1 quarter if you help rake the leaves. Your neighbor will give you 1 quarter if you walk his dog. If you do everything, will you have enough money for the balloon?

2 You can add to find out how much you will make.

3 **Think:** How much will you make for folding the clothes? You will make 1 quarter.
Think: How much will you make for washing the car? You will make 1 quarter.
Think: How much will you make for walking the dog? You will make 1 quarter.
Think: How much will you make in all?
You will make 3 quarters in all. Three quarters is 75¢. That's enough for the balloon.

4 Why did you need to make money?
You wanted to buy a big balloon.
Did you make enough money to buy it? Yes.

Distribute **Math Center Card 2A** to children.

Math Center Card 2A

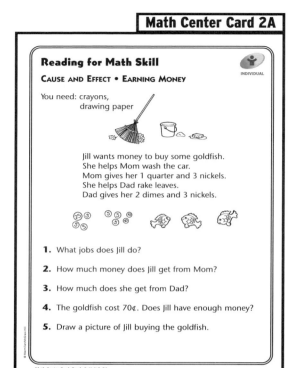

Reading for Math Skill

CAUSE AND EFFECT • EARNING MONEY

You need: crayons, drawing paper

Jill wants money to buy some goldfish.
She helps Mom wash the car.
Mom gives her 1 quarter and 3 nickels.
She helps Dad rake leaves.
Dad gives her 2 dimes and 3 nickels.

1. What jobs does Jill do?

2. How much money does Jill get from Mom?

3. How much does she get from Dad?

4. The goldfish cost 70¢. Does Jill have enough money?

5. Draw a picture of Jill buying the goldfish.

Math Center Card, Grade 2, Unit 2, 2A

STRATEGY: Act It Out

Model the strategy using a word problem such as the following:

 Read Max has 8 bottle caps. His mom gives him two more. How many does he have in all?

 Plan I can count on from 8 to find out how many bottle caps Max has. I can use cubes to act it out.

 Solve I start with 8 cubes. Then I add 2 more cubes. Now I'll count the cubes. There are 10 cubes in all. Max must have 10 bottle caps.

Look Back I'll check my answer again. This time I'll count on 2 starting from 8. 8, 9, 10. 8 + 2 =10.
Does my answer make sense? Yes.

Distribute **Math Center Card 2B** to children.

Math Center Card 2B

Problem Solving: Strategy

ACT IT OUT • HOW MANY WAYS?

PARTNERS

You need: quarters, dimes, nickels, pennies

Work with a partner. Act out each problem. Write the answers to the questions.

1. You want to buy a cup of lemonade for 20¢. How many different ways can you make 20¢? Write the ways.

2. You want to buy flowers for a friend. You have a half dollar, a dime, and a nickel. How much money do you have?
   How much money will you have left if you buy 3 flowers?

Math Center Card, Grade 2, Unit 2, 2B

Assessment Checklist

	STUDENT NAMES									
SCHOOL:										
TEACHER: **SCHOOL YEAR:**										
Mark: + = Mastery √ = Satisfactory – = Needs Improvement										
LEVEL OF LANGUAGE PROFICIENCY (1–5)										
MATH OBJECTIVES										
• Compare and order numbers to 100.										
• Identify coins and their values.										
• Identify place value for numbers to 100.										
• Estimate and compare numbers.										
• Identify odd and even numbers.										
ESL/TESOL LISTENING/SPEAKING										
Conduct transactions.										
Follow oral and written directions.										
Hypothesize and predict.										
Select, connect, and explain information.										
ESL/TESOL READING										
Read about subject matter information.										
Apply basic reading comprehension skills.										
Follow written directions, implicit and explicit.										
ESL WRITING										
Write to demonstrate comprehension.										
Use drawing or writing as appropriate to express understanding.										
Write using spelling patterns and targeted English vocabulary.										

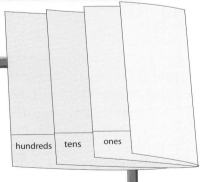

1 **Preproduction**
- Did children write the unit vocabulary?
- Did they copy the definitions?

2 **3** **Early Production and Speech Emergence**
- Did children label the tabs correctly?
- Did they write the vocabulary words?
- Did they copy the definitions?

4 **5** **Intermediate and Advanced Fluency**
- Did children write definitions for the unit vocabulary?
- Did they use correct spelling and grammar?

hundreds   tens   ones

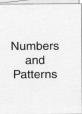

Numbers and Patterns

UNIT 3

Planner

Time, Graphs, and Regrouping

Assessment
p. 71
• Assessment Checklist
• Foldables

LOG ON Visit **www.mmhmath.com**

Unit Activities	
• **Activity 1** Grab Those Cubes! p. 54	• **Activity 3** Show the Time, p. 55
• **Activity 2** Regroup or Not? p. 54	• **Activity 4** Holidays of the Year, p. 55

Lessons	Key Objectives	Vocabulary	Materials	Resources
READ TOGETHER "Time Passes" by Ilo Orleans, pp. 52—53	**Math:** Explore the concept of time. **ESL/TESOL:** Goal 1, Standard 3.	day, hour, minute, pass, seconds, sixty, stand for, time, twenty-four		Graphic Organizer 1: Word Web
UNIT WARM-UP Understanding Time p. 56	**Math:** Tell and write time. Identify relationships of time. **ESL/TESOL:** Goal 1, Standard 3.	hour, hour hand, minute, minute hand	cardboard minute hand and hour hand, timepieces	**Overhead Manipulative:** Clock
LESSON 1 Time to the Hour and Half Hour pp. 58—59	**Math:** Tell and write time to the hour and half-hour. **ESL/TESOL:** Goal 1, Standard 3.	half hour, minute	crayons, paper, glue, scissors	Learning Resource 13 Teacher Tools 15 and 17
LESSON 2 Time to Five Minutes pp. 60—61	**Math:** Tell and write time to five minute intervals. **ESL/TESOL:** Goal 2/1, Standard 1/3.	quarter hour	clock, crayons, egg timer, index cards, scissors	Learning Resource 14
LESSON 3 Find Elapsed Time pp. 62—63	**Math:** Find elapsed time. Identify relationships of time. **ESL/TESOL:** Goal 2/1, Standard 1/3.	A.M., P.M.	paper, glue, index cards, number cards, plastic clock	Learning Resource 15 Teacher Tool 15
LESSON 4 Surveys pp. 64—65	**Math:** Record numerical data in systematic ways. **ESL/TESOL:** Goal 2/1, Standard 1/3.	chart, data, key, survey, tally mark	chart paper, markers, four clear plastic cups, straws	Learning Resource 16
LESSON 5 Make and Interpret Graphs pp. 66—67	**Math:** Read, interpret, and create graphs. **ESL/TESOL:** Goal 1, Standard 3.	bar graph, key, picture graph	assorted graphs, butcher paper, crayons, glue, index cards	Learning Resource 17
LESSON 6 Regrouping Numbers pp. 68—69	**Math:** Regroup numbers to add. Rename numbers in more than one way. **ESL/TESOL:** Goal 1, Standard 3.	regroup, total	connecting cubes, number cubes	Learning Resource 18 Teacher Tool 8
PROBLEM SOLVING p. 70 • Skill: Identify Extra Information • Strategy: Write an Equation	Use skills and strategies to solve problems.			**Math Center Cards 3A, 3B**

See **Math at Home Family Guide** for additional math vocabulary, activities, and games in English, Spanish, and Haitian Creole.

English Vocabulary

Dear Family: Please help your child practice the key vocabulary words for this unit.

bar graph a way of showing and comparing data using bars of different lengths

calendar a chart that shows the days, weeks, and months of the year

chart a table that lists information using numbers

data facts, numbers, or other kinds of information that has been gathered

pictograph a way of showing and comparing data using pictures

Vocabulario en español

Estimados familiares: Por favor ayuden a su hijo/a a practicar las palabras del vocabulario de esta unidad.

gráfica de barras manera de mostrar y comparar datos usando barras de distintos tamaños

calendario cuadro con los días, semanas y meses del año

tabla cuadro que da información usando números

datos hechos, números y otro tipo de información que se reúne

pictograma manera de mostrar y comparar datos usando ilustraciones

Vokabilè an kreyol

Chè paran: Tanpri ede pitit la pratike mo vokabilè nan seksyon sa a.

dyagram an band se yon fason pou prezante epi konpare done avèk band ki gen longè diferan

kalandriye se yon tablo ki montre jou, semèn ak mwa ki nan yon ane

tab enfòmasyon se yon tablo ki gen lis enfòmasyon yo prezante avèk nomb

done se evènman, nomb oswa lòt kalite enfòmasyon yo kolekte

piktogram se yon fason pou prezante epi konpare done yo mete nan tablo

Time Passes

by Ilo Orleans

 25 minutes

Math Objective
- Explore the concept of time.

ESL/TESOL Descriptors
- Listen to and imitate how others use English.
- Use context to construct meaning.

Reading Skill
- Recognize sequence of events.

Vocabulary
- day, hour, minute, pass, seconds, sixty, stand for, time, twenty-four

---

Before Reading

Build Background/Oral Language
Distribute the Graphic Organizer 1: Word Web. Display various timepieces to children and ask them to write as many time words as they can on their web. Ask children to read their words aloud as you make a giant word web on the board.

During Reading

- Read the poem to the class. Encourage children to ask about difficult words. Then make this chart on the board:

  60 seconds = 1 minute   24 hours = 1 day

  60 minutes = 1 hour   365 days = 1 year

- Direct attention to the classroom clock and point to the lines that mark minutes. Explain that each line stands for the start of a new minute.

- Reread the poem line by line. Have children repeat each line after you. Then reread the poem in unison.

Phonological/Phonemic Awareness
Draw attention to the word ending-*ty* in the words *sixty* and *twenty*. Ask children to name other number words with this ending and list them on the board.

After Reading

Help children recognize the sequence of time events by asking: ***Which is the shortest: a second, an hour, or a minute? Which is the longest? Can you put them in order from shortest to longest?***

Art Have each child draw a clock that shows the time a favorite activity begins. Invite children to write a few sentences about the activity and how long it takes. Collect and display the drawings.

Assessment

Observe students' participation and fluency as you read and discuss the poem together. See Assessment Checklist on page 71.

Multilevel Strategies

1 Preproduction
Say: ***Underline the number words in the poem.***

Writing Have children copy the number words *sixty* and *twenty*.

2 3 Early Production and Speech Emergence
Ask: ***What are the two number words in the poem?***

Writing Ask students to write all the number words that end in-*ty*.

4 5 Intermediate and Advanced Fluency
Ask: ***What number words can you say that end in-ty?***

Writing Ask students to write all the number words and circle the ones ending in-*ty*.

Time Passes

by Ilo Orleans

*Here is a little poem to help you
remember about minutes and hours and days.*

Sixty seconds
Pass in a minute.
Sixty minutes
Pass in an hour.
Twenty-four hours
Pass in a day—
And that's how TIME
Keeps passing away!

Activities

Readiness

ACTIVITY 1

SMALL GROUP

Grab Those Cubes!

- Copy the graph and fill in your names. Take turns.

- Take a handful of cubes and make a train. Color 1 square for each cube.

- Use the graph to answer the questions. Record the answers.

1. Who took the most cubes? The fewest cubes?

2. How many cubes did the group take in all?

YOU NEED

bag of inch graph paper

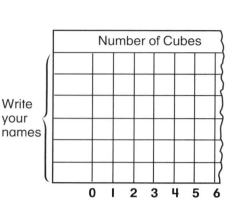

Number of Cubes

Write your names

0 1 2 3 4 5 6

Read and Create Graphs

ACTIVITY 2

INDIVIDUAL

Regroup or Not?

- Mix up the cards. Put them facedown on the table.

- Pick 1 card. Take that many ones models.

- Pick another card. Take that many tens.

- Regroup. Trade 10 ones for 1 ten. Trade 10 tens for 1 hundred.

- Write how many hundreds, tens, and ones. Write the number.

Play 4 more times.

YOU NEED

number cards

20 [cube train]

20 [cube]

| 14 | Tens | 11 | Ones = |

1 Hundred 5 Tens 1 Ones = 151

Regroup Numbers to Add

© Macmillan/McGraw-Hill

Activities

Game Zone

ACTIVITY 3

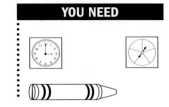
SMALL GROUP

Show the Time

Show 12 o'clock on the clock.

Take turns.

YOU NEED

- Spin.

- Tell how many minutes the spinner shows.

- Add your minutes to the time on the clock. Write the new time. Draw your clock.

Play until someone reaches 6 o'clock.

12:15

Identify Relationships of Time

INDIVIDUAL

ACTIVITY 4

Holidays of the Year

Use a calendar.

YOU NEED

12-month calendar

- Find 10 holidays in the year.

- Write the date of each holiday. Write the day of the week, too.

- Write the dates in order from January through December.

Read a Calendar

© Macmillan/McGraw-Hill

Warm-Up

 30 minutes

▶ **Key Strategy**
Use visuals

▶ **Format**
Whole class and student pairs

▶ **Math Vocabulary**
hour, hour hand, minute, minute hand

▶ **Daily Vocabulary**
after, before, clock, clock face, diary, digital, egg timer, hourglass, numeral, stopwatch, timepiece

▶ **Resource**
Overhead Manipulative:
Clock

▶ **Materials**
calendar, cardboard minute hand and hour hand, clocks (analog and digital), egg timer, large precut circle, markers, paper fastener, stopwatch

LOG
ON
Visit **www.mmhmath.com**
to find printable
Vocabulary Cards
that help build
academic language.

Understanding Time

Math Objectives	ESL/TESOL Descriptors
■ Tell and write time.	■ Use context to construct meaning.
■ Identify relationships of time.	■ Practice new language.

Activate Prior Knowledge Pass around various timepieces: watch, stopwatch, egg timer, calendar, etc. Ask children what they know about these timepieces and telling time. Write vocabulary words on the board. Ask: **How are these timepieces the same?** *(all record and measure time)* Help children to begin a Word Wall display about time.

Hands-on Lesson Display a big circle to use as a clock face. You may want to use **Overhead Manipulatives:** Clock. Explain that clocks tell time in hours, minutes, and sometimes seconds. Elicit from children that 60 seconds = 1 minute and 60 minutes = 1 hour.

● Invite children to help you label the clock face with numerals. Draw the lines that mark the minutes and explain that each line marks the start of a minute. Fasten the minute hand and hour hand to the clock.

● Review the parts of a clock. As you point to each part, elicit from children its name. *(clock face, numeral, minute hand, hour hand)*

● Move the minute hand around the clock slowly as you invite the children to count the minute lines to 60. Point out the five-minute increments between each numeral and ask children to skip-count by fives to 60. When they have finished, demonstrate the slow movement of the hour hand as the minutes pass.

● Invite children to take turns telling time to the hour. Put the minute hand on 12. Then have volunteers move the hour hand to show different times. Encourage each volunteer to ask: **What time is it?**

● Model different ways to write and say a time: *One o'clock; 1:00; It's one o'clock; It's one.*

Multilevel Strategies

1 Preproduction
Say different times for children to model on the big clock.

2 3 Early Production and Speech Emergence
Model different times on the clock and ask children to tell you the time.

4 5 Intermediate and Advanced Fluency
Model different times on the clock and ask children to say the time and describe the position of the hands.

Procedure: Help children make these Foldables to write vocabulary words and definitions throughout the unit. Encourage children to use the Foldables as a study guide.

Layered-Look Book

1. Provide each child with two sheets of 11" × 17" paper, or use two 6-foot-long sheets of bulletin board paper to make one large classroom Layered-Look Book.

2. Place the sheets of paper an equal distance apart.

3. Roll the bottom of the two sheets up to make three tabs the same size. Fold staple, and label the tabs as illustrated.

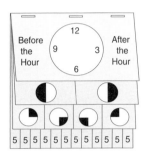

4. Include math words, clock faces, student notes, examples, and illustrations of time problems under the tabs.

Going Further Children can use their Layered-Look Book to review telling time by comparing their pictures and examples. Children may also want to organize a sequence of events chart to keep track of time during their day at school.

Folded Chart

1. Fold a sheet of 11" × 17" or 12" × 18" paper in half like a hot dog.

2. Open and make a 1" fold along one of the short sides.

3. Trace along the fold lines to make a chart with two columns.

4. Children can make as many charts as needed to work through the lessons. Teach children how to make their own charts and use them to demonstrate data collecting.

5. Children may want to draw a picture of the data they have collected. They can use this drawing to represent a survey they conduct.

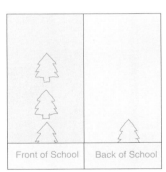

Front of School | Back of School

Going Further Children can use the Folded Chart to review by making inferences about different strategies presented throughout the unit. They can also create another Folded Chart to make a line graph from the same or different sets of data.

45 minutes

▶ **Key Strategy**
Use visuals

▶ **Format**
Whole class and student pairs

▶ **Math Vocabulary**
half hour, minute

▶ **Daily Vocabulary**
activities, after, before, schedule

▶ **Resources**
Learning Resource 13
Teacher Tools 15 and 17

Materials
- crayons or markers
- drawing paper
- glue
- heavy paper
- scissors

Assessment

Check children's mastery of the lesson vocabulary by observing them as they complete the lesson. See Assessment Checklist on page 71. Remind students to work on their Foldables.

Home Connection

Invite children to make a Saturday schedule with a family member and share it with the class.

Time to the Hour and Half Hour

Math Objective	**ESL/TESOL Descriptors**
■ Tell and write time to the hour and half hour.	■ Use context to construct meaning. ■ Practice new language.

Activate Prior Knowledge Ask students what they know about telling time. Ask: *Why is it important to tell time?* Role-play situations showing the importance of telling time: being late, burning a cake, missing the bus, and so on.

Hands-on Lesson Make a sample "School Day Schedule." Ask: *What time do you get up? What time do you go to school?* and so on. Write activities and starting times to the hour or half hour. Ask children to repeat the times.

- Use Teacher Tool 15: Analog Clock Face to make clocks. Ask: *How many minutes are in an hour?* Show that half of one hour is 30 minutes. Ask children to look at the schedule and show the activity starting times on their clocks.

- Write *10:30* and ask a child to read it. Say: *Two ways to say 10:30 are ten thirty and 30 minutes after 10.* Ask: *Which activity on our schedule begins at 30 minutes after the hour?*

- Have pairs draw two activities that begin on the hour or half hour. Then hand out Teacher Tool 17: Clock Cards Without Times. Explain that _:30 shows the half hour on a digital clock. Ask one child to draw hands on the clocks to show when an activity begins as the other writes the time on the digital clocks. Have them glue the clocks on their pictures.

- Distribute Learning Resource 13. Have children match the clocks and times.

Challenge Give Teacher Tool 15 to pairs. Have children take turns showing a time to the hour and asking their partner: *What time will it be a half hour from now?*

Multilevel Strategies

1 Preproduction
Say times on the hour and half hour and ask students to model them on their analog clock face. Say: *Show me (six thirty).*

Writing Ask children to write the times that you say.

2 3 Early Production and Speech Emergence
Use a clock face to model times on the hour and half hour and ask: *What time is it?*

Writing Say a time and ask children to write it two different ways.

4 5 Intermediate and Advanced Fluency
Model times on the hour and half hour and ask children to tell the time and describe the positions of the clock hands.

Writing Ask children to write the time and a sentence describing the hands' position.

Name _____

Matching Times

Match the clocks and the times.

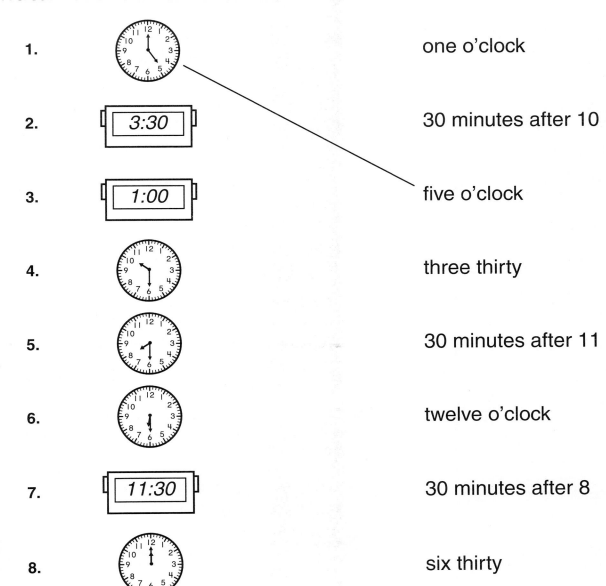

1. one o'clock

2. 3:30 30 minutes after 10

3. 1:00 five o'clock

4. three thirty

5. 30 minutes after 11

6. twelve o'clock

7. 11:30 30 minutes after 8

8. six thirty

Write the half hour that comes next.

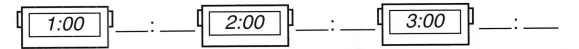

1:00 ___ : ___   2:00 ___ : ___   3:00 ___ : ___

▶ **Key Strategy**
Use visuals

▶ **Format**
Whole class, student pairs, small groups

▶ **Math Vocabulary**
quarter hour

▶ **Daily Vocabulary**
after, before, estimate, how long, more, quarter, takes

▶ **Resources**
Learning Resource 14
Teacher Tool 15

Materials
- big clock from Warm-Up
- crayons (4 colors)
- egg timer (5 minutes)
- index cards
- markers
- scissors

Assessment

Check children's mastery of the lesson vocabulary by observing them as they complete the lesson. See Assessment Checklist on page 71. Remind students to work on their Foldables.

Home Connection

Have children take home their Learning Resource page to share with family members. Invite them to draw a time path of their own to share.

Time to Five Minutes

Math Objective	**ESL/TESOL Descriptors**
■ Tell and write time to 5-minute intervals.	■ Participate in full class, group, and pair discussions.
	■ Practice new language.

Activate Prior Knowledge Display a clock and ask children to name the parts. Ask: *What do the lines between the numbers measure? How long does it take for the minute hand to move from one number to the next number?* Start at 12 and ask children to count by fives around the clock.

Hands-on Lesson Invite children to help you make a list of activities that take about five minutes. Ask small groups to choose an activity. If there are none that can be done in the classroom, suggest that five groups draw a picture or build a block tower. Ask a volunteer to set a timer for five minutes.

- When the time is up, ask groups if they completed their activity. If not, ask them to estimate how much longer it will take. *Will it take (5, 10, 15) more minutes?*

- Display the time to the nearest 5-minute interval on the clock. Ask: *If it takes (5, 10, 15) more minutes to finish a drawing, what time will it be?* Write times and ask a child to show the new time on the clock.

- Ask: *Is there another way to say 15 minutes?* (quarter hour) Color each **quarter hour** on the big clock a different color. Ask: *How many quarters are in one hour? What does **quarter after** mean? What does **quarter to** mean?* Model different ways to write time to the quarter hour.

- Have children complete Learning Resource 14: Mixed-Up Clocks.

Challenge Give pairs Teacher Tool 15: Analog Clock Face. Ask children to take turns showing a time to five minutes and asking: *What time will it be in (10, 15, 20) minutes?*

Multilevel Strategies

1 Preproduction
Say a time, write it, and have children show it on the big clock.

Writing Show a time on the big clock. Write it down and have children copy it.

2 3 Early Production and Speech Emergence
Show a time on the big clock and ask: *What time is it?*

Writing Show a time on the big clock and have students write the time in two ways.

4 5 Intermediate and Advanced Fluency
Show a time on the big clock. Ask children to say the time and an activity they might do then.

Writing Ask children to write the time and write about the activity.

14

Name _____

Mixed-Up Clocks

Cut out each box and put the times in order.

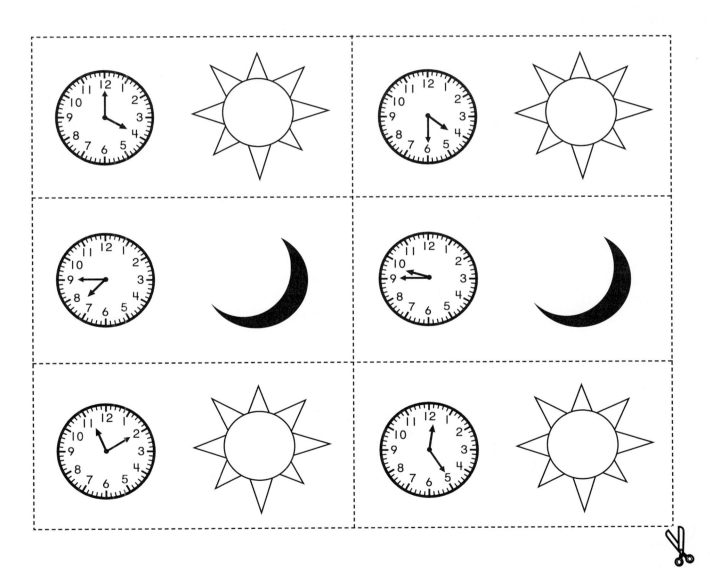

 45 minutes

▶ **Key Strategy**
Use visuals

▶ **Format**
Whole class and groups

▶ **Math Vocabulary**
A.M., P.M.

▶ **Daily Vocabulary**
afternoon, midnight, morning, night, noon

▶ **Resources**
Learning Resource 15
Teacher Tool 15

Materials
- 11 × 14-inch paper
- glue
- index cards
- number cards (1–6)
- plastic clock

Assessment

Check students' mastery of the lesson vocabulary by observing them as they complete the lesson. See Assessment Checklist on page 71. Remind students to work on their Foldables.

Home Connection

Have students make calendars to share with family members. Invite students to work with family members to include birthdays or other important events, then share with the class.

Find Elapsed Time

Math Objectives	**ESL/TESOL Descriptors**
■ Find elapsed time.	■ Negotiate and manage interaction to accomplish tasks.
■ Identify relationships of time.	■ Practice new language.

Activate Prior Knowledge Display assorted timepieces such as a clock, a watch, an egg timer, a calendar, a stopwatch, etc. Ask children to recall what they know about measuring and telling time.

Hands-on Lesson Write A.M. and P.M. Explain A.M. means the hours from midnight until noon, and P.M. means the hours from noon until midnight, but that we also describe time with the words *morning, afternoon,* and *night.*

- Display two clocks with movable hands. Ask a child to show 9:00 A.M. on one clock. Ask: **How can I make the other clock show the time two hours later?** Ask: **Which clock hand will I use?** *(hour hand)* Model the activity. Say: **I count on two hours.** Count as you move the hands and ask: **What is the time?** Ask for volunteers to repeat this activity using other start and finish times.

- Hand out Teacher Tool 15: Analog Clock Face to pairs and ask children to make clocks.

- Give each pair six cards. Ask them to write a time to the half hour on 3 cards. On the second group of cards, ask them to write 1, 2, and 3 hours.

- Have pairs put cards in two piles. Ask the children to take turns picking a card from each pile and telling how much time has passed. Encourage students to use their clocks to help them model the answer. Then hand out Learning Resource 15: What Is the Time? for children to complete.

Challenge Invite students to create picture stories about a favorite activity. Ask them to include a start and finish time by writing the times or drawing pictures of clock faces.

 **Multilevel Strategies**

1 Preproduction
Ask children to show 3:00 on the clock and then show the clock after two hours have passed.

Writing Ask students to write the start and finish times.

2 3 Early Production and Speech Emergence
Display 3:00 and then move the hands to show 5:00. Ask children how much time has passed.

Writing Ask children to write the start and finish times and how much time has passed.

4 5 Intermediate and Advanced Fluency
Ask children to make up a question for a partner. For example: *It's 4:00. Two hours passed. What time is it?*

Writing Ask pairs to write their problems for another pair to solve.

Name _____

What Is the Time?

Write the start time. Then draw the finish time on the clock.

START TIME	TIME PASSED	FINISH TIME
_____ : _____	2 hours	
1:00 _____ : _____	1 hour	⬚ : ⬚
_____ : _____	4 hours	
12:30 _____ : _____	3 hours	⬚ : ⬚

 45 minutes

▶ **Key Strategy**
Use visuals

▶ **Format**
Whole class and small groups

▶ **Math Vocabulary**
chart, key, survey, tally mark

▶ **Daily Vocabulary**
best, data, favorite, gather information, least, results, vote

▶ **Resource**
Learning Resource 16

Materials
- chart paper
- crayons or markers
- four clear plastic cups
- straws

Assessment

Check students' mastery of the lesson vocabulary by observing them as they complete the lesson. See page 71 for Assessment Checklist. Remind students to work on their Foldables.

Home Connection

Have students take home the Learning Resource to share with family members. Invite children to ask family members to name their favorite animal so they can share the information with their class and make a new survey.

Surveys

Math Objectives	**ESL/TESOL Descriptors**
■ Record numerical data in systematic ways.	■ Follow oral and written directions, implicit and explicit.
■ Represent the same data set in more than one way.	■ Use context to construct meaning.

Activate Prior Knowledge Put four cups on a table with labels: green, blue, yellow, orange. Give each child a straw. Ask: *Which of these colors is your favorite? Put your straw in your favorite color cup.* Tell children that this is a **survey.** Ask: *What does this survey tell us?*

Hands-on Lesson Write the word *survey* and explain that people take surveys to collect **data,** or information. Ask: *How can we show the results of our survey?* Explain that one way to show the data is to count the votes and show them on a tally **chart.**

- Make a **tally mark** on the board and write the term. Explain the **key** that one tally mark = one vote. Show children how to record five tally marks. Hand out Learning Resource 16: Survey-Rama.

- Ask four children to count the number of votes for each color. Ask children to make tally marks on their charts to show the totals. Ask: *Do you know a fast way to count all the tallies?* (yes, skip-count by fives and count on by ones)

- Ask children to count the tallies to find the total number of votes for each color. Have them write the total next to the tally marks. Ask: *How can we compare the data?* (by looking at the total number of votes for each color) Ask questions such as: *Which color does the class like the best? The least?*

- Ask children to work with a partner to complete the worksheets. When they have completed the chart, invite children to share their answers.

Cultural Link Ask children to make up a survey about where their families come from.

Multilevel Strategies

1 Preproduction
Say: *Point to your favorite color on the tally chart.*

Writing Ask students to write the name of their favorite color on the tally chart.

2 3 Early Production and Speech Emergence
Ask students to name colors on the tally chart and say the totals.

Writing Have children write the colors and the total votes for each color.

4 5 Intermediate and Advanced Fluency
Ask: *What do the survey results tell us?*

Writing Ask children to write a list of steps for taking a survey.

Name _____

Survey-Rama

OUR FAVORITE COLOR		
	Tally	Total
green		
blue		
yellow		
orange		

1. Put a tally for each vote.

2. Add the tallies to find the total votes for each color.

3. Look at the chart and compare the totals for each color.

4. The survey results tell me _____

_____

_____

_____

_____

_____

45 minutes

▶ **Key Strategy**
Use visuals

▶ **Format**
Whole class and student pairs

▶ **Math Vocabulary**
bar graph, key, picture graph

▶ **Daily Vocabulary**
bird, cat, display, labels, rabbit, titles, turtle

▶ **Resource**
Learning Resource 17

Materials
- assorted graphs (bar graphs, picture graphs, line graphs, tally chart)
- butcher paper
- crayons or colored pencils
- glue or tape
- large index cards

Assessment

Check children's mastery of the lesson vocabulary by observing them as they complete the lesson. See page 71 for Assessment Checklist. Remind students to work on their Foldables.

Home Connection

Have children take home the Learning Resource to share. Have them ask their families what animal they would like to be and share the answers with the class.

Make and Interpret Graphs

Math Objectives	ESL/TESOL Descriptors
■ Read, interpret, and create graphs.	■ Use context to construct meaning.
■ Record numerical data in systemic ways.	■ Practice new language.

Activate Prior Knowledge Show children a tally chart, such as the one from Lesson 4. Ask: *What kind of chart is this? Why is it useful to put data in a chart like this? (You can see it quickly.)* Pass around a variety of graphs, e.g., **bar graphs, picture graphs**, and line graphs. Tell children these are other ways to show data. Point out that how the data is displayed tells us the type of graph it is.

Hands-on Lesson Hand out large index cards. Sketch a bird, a cat, a turtle, and a rabbit. Ask: *Imagine you could be an animal. Which animal would you be?* Invite children to draw the animal and put their name on the card. Tell children they will use the cards to make a picture graph.

- Use a large piece of paper or bulletin board to set up a picture graph. Ask children to help you write a title, labels, and **key.** Then invite students to glue or tape their animal cards next to the appropriate animal name. Then ask: *How many children want to be birds? Cats? Turtles? Rabbits?* When the graph is complete, encourage them to make comparisons.

- Say: *We can show the same data in a bar graph.* Set up the graph. Give children a paper square and ask them to color the squares red for bird, blue for cat, yellow for turtle, and green for rabbit. Have children glue their squares on the bar graph. Encourage them to make comparisons when the graph is complete.

- Hand out Learning Resource 17: Fun with Graphs for children to complete.

Challenge Collect and display data about children's favorite foods in a tally chart. Challenge children to show the data in another way.

Multilevel Strategies

❶ Preproduction
Ask children to point to the row showing cats on the graph.

Writing Point to the picture graph. Ask children to write how many children wanted to be birds.

❷❸ Early Production and Speech Emergence
Point to a graph and ask: *How many children want to be birds?*

Writing Ask children to write one thing that the picture graph tells us.

❹❺ Intermediate and Advanced Fluency
Ask children what they can learn by looking at the picture or graphs.

Writing Ask children to write about what they can learn by looking at the picture or bar graphs.

Name _____

Fun with Graphs

Look at the class picture graph and the bar graph.
Then answer the questions.

1. What is the title of the picture graph?

_____

2. Did more children want to be a bird or a cat?

_____

3. How many children want to be a turtle?

_____

4. How many bars are on the bar graph?

_____

5. How many children does one picture represent?

Each picture = ____ person.

Lesson 6

🕐 **45 minutes**

▶ **Key Strategy**
Use manipulatives

▶ **Format**
Whole class and student pairs

▶ **Math Vocabulary**
regroup, total

▶ **Daily Vocabulary**
trading

▶ **Resources**
Learning Resource 18
Teacher Tool 8

Materials
- connecting cubes
- number cubes
- 2-digit number cards for pairs

Assessment

Check children's mastery of the lesson vocabulary by observing them as they complete the lesson. See page 71 for Assessment Checklist. Remind students to work on their Foldables.

Home Connection

Have children take home Learning Resource 18 to share with family members. Invite children to show family members how they can model different numbers using dimes and pennies.

Regrouping Numbers

Math Objectives	**ESL/TESOL Descriptors**
■ Regroup numbers to add.	■ Use context to construct meaning.
■ Rename numbers in more than one way.	■ Practice new language.

Activate Prior Knowledge Ask children when they use groups of ten. *(Answers will vary, but will likely include skip-counting.)* Ask children to skip-count by tens to 100. Then display a hundred chart and use it to practice adding tens. Ask children to point to numbers between 10 and 80. Have children count on 1 ten, 2 tens, or 3 tens.

Hands-on Lesson Use connecting cubes and Teacher Tool 8: Place-Value Workmat to show 16 as 1 ten and 6 ones. Tell children that when they have more than 10 ones, they can trade the ones for a ten. This is called **regrouping.**

- Give pairs 9 tens, 20 ones, and a place-value mat. Have them roll number cubes to make 2-digit numbers. Have each pair represent these numbers with cubes, first as ones, and then by regrouping to tens and ones.

- Model adding 28 + 6. Ask: **How many tens?** Ask: **How many ones?** *(14)* Ask: **Can you regroup?** *(yes, because there are more than ten ones)* Model regrouping 10 ones as a ten, moving the ten to the appropriate column. Ask: **How many ones are left?** *(4)* **How many tens are there?** *(3)* **What is the total?** *(34)* Have children roll the number cubes to create similar addition sentences to solve.

- Next, model adding 16 + 29 by repeating the activity above. Have children roll the number cubes four times to get two 2-digit numbers. Ask them to make vertical addition sentences, then use connecting cubes to show each number. Have them line up the models to parallel the addition sentence and then solve the problem.

- Then hand out Learning Resource 18: Show That Number! for children to complete.

Challenge Have pairs write and trade story problems with 2-digit numbers.

Multilevel Strategies

1 Preproduction
Write various addition sentences and ask children to nod if they need to regroup.

Writing Say a 2-digit number and ask children to write how many tens and ones are in it.

2 3 Early Production and Speech Emergence
Write various addition sentences and ask children if they need to regroup.

Writing Ask children to write *regroup* or *don't regroup.*

4 5 Intermediate and Advanced Fluency
Invite children to explain how they decide if they need to regroup.

Writing Ask children to write a letter to a friend about what they have learned.

Name _____

Show That Number!

Look at the different ways to show the same number.
Write how many tens and ones are in each box.

1.

tens	ones

tens	ones

tens	ones

___3___ ___4___   ___ ___   ___ ___

2.

tens	ones

tens	ones

tens	ones

___ ___   ___ ___   ___ ___

Show each number another way.

3.

tens	ones	tens	ones

tens	ones	tens	ones

___1___ ___0___ ___ ___   ___4___ ___2___ ___ ___

Problem Solving
Reading for Math

Remind students of
the basic steps
of problem solving.

SKILL: Identify Extra Information
Model the skill using a word problem such as the
following:

1 Karen has 4 goldfish in her fish tank. She went to
the pet store to buy more fish. She saw 3 puppies
and 4 kittens. She bought 6 more gold fish. How
many fish does she have now?

2 I can add to find the number of fish Karen has
now.

3 **Think:** How many fish did Karen have in her tank?
Karen had 4 goldfish.
Think: How many goldfish did Karen buy? 6 more.
I can carry out my plan. $4 + 6 = 10$
Karen now has 10 goldfish.

4 What was the **important information?**
The number of goldfish Karen had at home and the
number of goldfish she bought.
What was **extra information** she didn't need to know?
The number of puppies and kittens at the store.

Distribute **Math Center Card 3A** to children.

Math Center Card 3A

Reading for Math Skill
SEQUENCE OF EVENTS • MY DAY
INDIVIDUAL

You need: clock

1. Make a list of what you do each day. Write a time for
each activity. Copy and complete these sentences.

I wake up at _____.
I get to school at _____.
I get home from school at _____.
I eat dinner at _____.
I go to bed at _____.

2. Draw clocks to show each time. Use a real clock to help
you.

Math Center Card, Grade 2, Unit 3, 3A

STRATEGY: Write an Equation
Model the strategy using a word problem such as
the following:

Read Marilyn wants to finish reading her book by tomorrow. She has read 73 pages. The book is 98 pages
long. How many more pages does she have to read?

Plan I can write a number sentence to solve the problem.

Solve **Think:** Do I add or subtract to find the answer?
I know the total number of pages and I know the
number of pages already read. I can subtract to
find how many more pages she has to read.
I can carry out my plan. $98 - 73 = 25$
Marilyn has 25 more pages to read.

Look Back Does my answer make sense? Yes.
How do I know?
I can add to check. $25 + 73 = 98$

Distribute **Math Center Card 3B** to children.

Math Center Card 3B

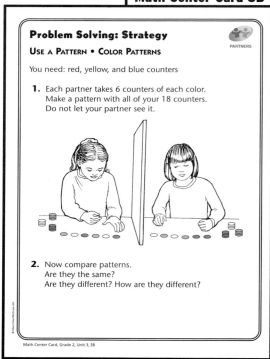

Problem Solving: Strategy
USE A PATTERN • COLOR PATTERNS
PARTNERS

You need: red, yellow, and blue counters

1. Each partner takes 6 counters of each color.
Make a pattern with all of your 18 counters.
Do not let your partner see it.

2. Now compare patterns.
Are they the same?
Are they different? How are they different?

Math Center Card, Grade 2, Unit 3, 3B

Assessment Checklist

	STUDENT NAMES										
SCHOOL:											
TEACHER: **SCHOOL YEAR:**											
Mark: + = Mastery ✓ = Satisfactory − = Needs Improvement											
LEVEL OF LANGUAGE PROFICIENCY (1–5)											
MATH OBJECTIVES											
• Explore the concept of time and elapsed time.											
• Read, interpret, and create graphs.											
• Regroup numbers to add.											
• Rename numbers in more than one way.											
• Represent the same data set in more than one way.											
• Tell and write time to the hour and half-hour.											
ESL/TESOL LISTENING/SPEAKING											
Listen to and imitate how others use English.											
Negotiate and manage interaction to accomplish tasks.											
Participate in full class, group, and pair discussions.											
Practice new language.											
Use context to construct meaning.											
ESL/TESOL READING											
Read about subject matter information.											
Apply basic reading comprehension skills.											
Follow written directions, implicit and explicit.											
ESL WRITING											
Write to demonstrate comprehension.											
Write using spelling patterns and targeted English vocabulary.											

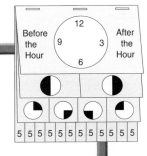

1 **Preproduction**
- Did children write the unit vocabulary?
- Did they copy the definitions?

2 **3** **Early Production and Speech Emergence**
- Did children label the tabs correctly?
- Did they write the vocabulary words?
- Did they copy the definitions?

4 **5** **Intermediate and Advanced Fluency**
- Did children write definitions for the unit vocabulary?
- Did they use correct spelling and grammar?

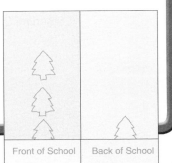

UNIT 4

Planner

Add and Subtract 2-Digit Numbers

Assessment
p. 93
• Assessment Checklist
• Foldables

LOG ON Visit **www.mmhmath.com**

Planner

Unit Activities	
• **Activity 1** *Readiness* Blue and Yellow, p. 76	• **Activity 3** Greatest Number Wins, p. 77
• **Activity 2** Number Roll, p. 76	• **Activity 4** Working Backward, p. 77

Lessons	Key Objectives	Vocabulary	Materials	Resources
READ TOGETHER "Band-Aids" by Shel Silverstein pp. 74–75	**Math:** Add a 1-digit number and a 2-digit number with and without regrouping. **ESL/TESOL:** Goal 1, Standard 3.	band-aid, body parts (ankle, etc.)		
UNIT WARM-UP Understanding Tens and Ones p. 78	**Math:** Add a 1-digit number and a 2-digit number without regrouping. **ESL/TESOL:** Goal 2, Standard 2.	addend, digits, number sentence, sum	cubes, tens and ones models (base-ten sets)	**Overhead Manipulatives** Teacher Tool 7
LESSON 1 Add Tens and Ones pp. 80–81	**Math:** Add a 1-digit number and a 2-digit number. **ESL/TESOL:** Goal 2/1, Standard 3/2.	count on, regroup, tens	tens and ones models (base-ten set)	Learning Resource 19 Teacher Tools 3, 8
LESSON 2 Add 2-Digit Numbers pp. 82–83	**Math:** Add two 2-digit numbers, with and without regrouping. **ESL/TESOL:** Goal 1/2, Standard 3/1.	addend, regroup	index cards with 2-digit addition exercises, tens and ones models	Learning Resource 20 Teacher Tools 7, 8
LESSON 3 Subtract Tens and Ones pp. 84–85	**Math:** Subtract a 1-digit number from a 2-digit number, with and without regrouping. **ESL/TESOL:** Goal 1, Standard 3.	count back, difference, number sentence, regroup	tens and ones models (base-ten set)	Learning Resource 21 Teacher Tools 3, 8
LESSON 4 Subtract 2-Digit Numbers pp. 86–87	**Math:** Subtract 2-digit numbers, with and without regrouping. **ESL/TESOL:** Goal 1/2, Standard 3/1.	addend, difference, regroup	index cards with subtractions, tens and ones models	Learning Resource 22 Teacher Tools 7, 8
LESSON 5 Estimate Sums and Differences pp. 88–89	**Math:** Estimate sums and differences. **ESL/TESOL:** Goal 2/1, Standard 1/3.	estimate, reasonable, round down, round up	butcher paper, index cards, markers	Learning Resource 23
LESSON 6 Add Three Addends pp. 90–91	**Math:** Add three 2-digit numbers. **ESL/TESOL:** Goal 2/1, Standard 2/3.	addend, double, sum	index cards with 2-digit numbers	Learning Resource 24
PROBLEM SOLVING p. 92 • Skill: Draw a Pattern • Strategy: Choose the Operation	Use skills and strategies to solve problems			**Math Center Cards 4A, 4B**

See **Math at Home Guide** for addtional math vocabulary, activities, and games in English, Spanish, and Haitian Creole.

English Vocabulary

Dear Family: Please help your child practice the key vocabulary words for this unit.

count back to start with the first number in a subtraction and count backward the number that is subtracted from it

estimate to make a close guess, for example, by rounding numbers in a math problem to the nearest ten

number sentence a complete math statement such as an addition or subtraction sentence, with the answer

reasonable answer to check if the sum is reasonable by rounding the addends to the greatest digit

regroup to change 10 ones to 1 ten or 1 ten to 10 ones to help with addition or subtraction

round to rewrite a number as the nearest ten, hundred, or so on

sum the result or total when you add two or more numbers

Vocabulario en español

Estimados familiares: Por favor ayuden a su hijo/a a practicar las palabras del vocabulario de esta unidad.

contar hacia atrás empezar a partir del primer número en una resta y contar hacia hacia atrás el número que se le resta

estimar adivinar una cantidad, por ejemplo, redondear los números a su decena más próxima

oración numérica enunciado matemático completo, por ejemplo una oración de suma o de resta con la respuesta

respuesta razonable comprobar si la suma tiene sentido redondeando los sumandos al dígito mayor

reagrupar convertir 10 unidades en 1 decena o 1 decena en 10 unidades para facilitar la suma o la resta

redondear escribir un número a la decena más próxima, a la centena más próxima, y así sucesivamente

suma el resultado o total que se obtiene al sumar dos o más números

---

Vokabilè an kreyol

Chè paran: Tanpri ede pitit la pratike mo vokabilè nan seksyon sa a.

konte nan lòd dekwasan vle di kòmanse avèk on premye nonb epi kòmanse konte pa bak

estimasyon se fè yon sipozisyon ki trè pwòch, pa egzanp lè w awondi nonb yo nan pwoblèm matematik pou fè yo rive nan dizèn ki pi pwòch la

fraz nimerik se yon fraz okonplè tankou yon fraz adisyon oswa soustraksyon avèk repons lan

repons ki fè sans se pou tcheke si sòm nan jistifye; Pou fè sa w ap awondi nonm ajoute yo a chif ki gen plis valè ya

regwoupe se chanje 10 inite an 1 dizèn pou sa kab ede nan adisyon

awondi se re-ekri yon nonb sou fòm dizèn santèn oswa kontinye nan menm fason

sòm se rezilta oswa total lè ou adisyone 2 oswa plis nonb

© Macmillan/McGraw-Hill

Band-Aids

by Shel Silverstein

 30 minutes

Math Objective
- Add a 1-digit number and a 2-digit number with and without regrouping.

ESL/TESOL Descriptor
- Listen to and imitate how others use English.

Reading Skill
- Draw conclusions

Vocabulary
ankle, Band-Aid, belly, bottom, chin, elbow, 'em, eye, finger, forehead, heel, knee, neck, nose, pity, shoulder, sore, toes, thigh, wrist

Before Reading

Build Background/Oral Language
Sketch a person on the board and review the words for body parts. Write the words on sticky notes and invite children to put them onto the appropriate place. Hand out the Graphic Organizer Word Web and ask children to write the words on it.

During Reading

- Read the poem through slowly, using gestures to reinforce the meaning. Encourage children to ask about new or difficult words.
- Invite the class to estimate how many Band-Aids the boy is wearing.
- Reread the poem line by line and ask children to repeat each line after you. Then ask children to make a tally mark for each Band-Aid. Count the tallies to find the total number, and compare the class estimate with the actual count. Compare that number to how many the boy has in the box of Band-Aids.
- Encourage a class discussion about why the boy is wearing so many Band-Aids. Introduce the words *conclude* and *conclusion* when the children have decided why the boy has so many Band-Aids. Then, read the poem again in unison.

Phonological/Phonemic Awareness
Draw attention to the word *knee*. Point out that in the initial consonant cluster /kn/ the *k* is silent. Have children repeat the word *knee* several times.

After Reading

Science Display a large precut outline of a child. Have volunteers read words from their word webs as other children draw Band-Aids on the body parts that are named in the poem.

Assessment

Observe children's participation as you reread the poem and make a tally chart of how many Band-Aids the boy is wearing. See Assessment Checklist on page 93.

Multilevel Strategies

1 Preproduction
Say: *Draw a circle around the number words in the poem.*

Writing Ask children to make a list of the number words in the poem.

2 3 Early Production and Speech Emergence
Say: *Tell me the numbers you hear in the poem.*

Writing Ask children to write the numbers of Band-Aids on each body part.

4 5 Intermediate and Advanced Fluency
Say: *Make up your own poem by changing the numbers. Read your poem to a partner.*

Writing Invite children to write the new poem and illustrate it.

Band-Aids

by Shel Silverstein

*There are a lot of Band-Aids in this classic poem,
but how many does this poor child need?*

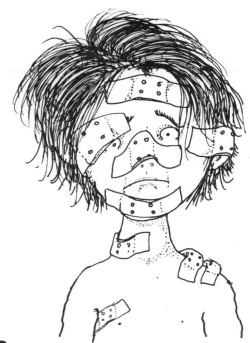

I have a Band-Aid on my finger,

One on my knee, and one on my nose,

One on my heel, and two on my shoulder,

Three on my elbow, and nine on my toes.

Two on my wrist, and one on my ankle,

One on my chin, and one on my thigh,

Four on my belly, and five on my bottom,

One on my forehead, and one on my eye.

One on my neck, and in case I might need 'em

I have a box full of thirty-five more.

But oh! I do think it's sort of a pity

I don't have a cut or a sore!

Activities

Readiness

PARTNERS

ACTIVITY 1

Blue and Yellow

The blue cards are tens. Stack them facedown.

The yellow cards are ones. Stack them facedown.

- Pick three cards from each stack.

- Use the cards to make three 2-digit numbers.

- Write an addition problem and find the sum.

- Trade your addition problem with your partner and show the work with dimes and pennies.

YOU NEED

blue cards numbered 0–9

yellow cards numbered 0–9

play money: 15 dimes, 27 pennies

Add a 1-Digit Number and a 2-Digit Number

ACTIVITY 2

INDIVIDUAL

Number Roll

- Roll 2 number cubes. Write a 2-digit number.

- Roll again. Write another 2-digit number.

- Build the larger number with ⬚⬚⬚⬚⬚⬚ and ⬚.

- Take away the smaller number from the larger number. Regroup if you need to.

- How many are left?

Write the subtraction problem.

YOU NEED

2 [number cube] (1–6)

9 [rod]

20 [cube]

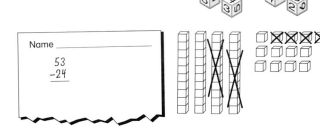

Name _____
53
−24

Subtract 2-Digit Numbers

76 Unit 4 · Activities

Activities

Game Zone

ACTIVITY 3

SMALL GROUP

Greatest Number Wins

Put the cards in a pile facedown.

YOU NEED

number cards with 2 digits

- Each player picks 3 cards.

- Find the sum of your 3 numbers.

- Check each other's answer.

- The player with the greatest sum gets 1 point.

Return the cards to the pile after each time.

The first player to get 5 points wins.

Add Three 2-Digit Numbers

PARTNERS

ACTIVITY 4

Working Backward

Take turns.

Do not let your partner see what you do.

YOU NEED

5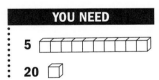

20 ▢

- Get some ▭ and ▢.

- Take some away. (You may want to regroup 1 ten as 10 ones before you take away.)

- Show your partner how many ▭ and ▢ you took away and how many are left.

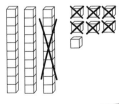
Name _____

- Ask your partner to tell how many ▭ and ▢ you started with.

Add 2-Digit Numbers

Understanding Tens and Ones

 30 minutes

▶ **Key Strategy**
Use manipulatives

▶ **Format**
Whole class

▶ **Math Vocabulary**
addend, digits, number sentence, sum

▶ **Daily Vocabulary**
model, organize

▶ **Resources**
Overhead Manipulatives:
base-ten-sets
Teacher Tool 7

▶ **Materials**
cubes, tens and ones models (base-ten sets)

Math Objective	ESL/TESOL Descriptors
▪ Add a 1-digit number and a 2-digit number without regrouping.	▪ Use context to construct meaning. ▪ Demonstrate knowledge through application in a variety of contexts.

Activate Prior Knowledge Help children to recall how many Band-Aids were in the boy's box in the poem "Band-Aids." *(35)* Ask: *How many tens are in this number?* *(3)* **How many ones?** *(5)* Hand out Teacher Tool 7: Place-Value Chart. Write 2-digit numbers on the board and ask children to write how many tens and ones are in each number in the place-value chart. You may want to use Base-Ten-Sets from **Overhead Manipulatives.**

Hands-on Lesson Display a pile of 30 cubes on a table. Ask a child to make a ten train and point out that a cube represents for one and a ten train represents 10 ones. Write *26* and *12* on the board. Ask: *How can you model 26 and 12 using tens and ones?*

● Invite a volunteer to organize the cubes into groups of tens and ones to make 26. Point out that organizing numbers with two **digits** into tens and ones can help them add.

● Invite another volunteer to organize the cubes into groups of tens and ones to make 12. Ask: *How can you organize the cubes to count?* Elicit from children that they can put the tens in one group and the ones in another group and then count by tens and ones.

● Invite volunteers to organize the groups and count. Ask: *What is the total?* *(38)* Write the **number sentence** *26 + 12 = 38* on the board and write **addend + addend = sum** underneath. Ask children to identify each addend and the sum.

● Repeat this activity using other 2-digit numbers where regrouping is not necessary.

Multilevel Strategies

1 **Preproduction**
Write 2-digit numbers and ask children to point to the tens and ones or say how many are in the number.

2 3 **Early Production and Speech Emergence**
Write 2-digit numbers and ask children to say how many tens and ones are in each.

4 5 **Intermediate and Advanced Fluency**
Have children write 2-digit numbers and ask a classmate to say how many tens and ones are in each.

 Visit **www.mmhmath.com** to find printable **Vocabulary Cards** that help build academic language.

Procedure: Help children make these Foldables to write vocabulary words and definitions throughout the unit. Encourage children to use the Foldables as a study guide.

Layered-Look Book

1. Provide each child with three sheets of 11" × 17" paper, or use three 6-foot-long sheets of bulletin-board paper to make one large classroom book.

2. Place the sheets of paper an equal distance apart as illustrated.

3. Roll the bottom of the three sheets up to make five tabs the same size. Fold, glue, and staple.

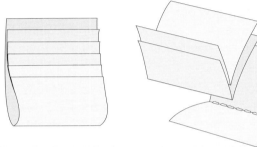

4. Have children record math words, symbols, and examples of 2-digit addition under the tabs of their Layered-Look Books.

Add and Subtract 2-Digit Numbers

| L1 |
| L2 |
| L3 |
| L4 |
| L5 |

Going Further
Children can use the Layered-Look Book to review by comparing their pictures and examples of 2-digit addition.

Accordion Book

1. Provide each child with three sheets of 11" × 17" paper.

2. Fold the three sheets of paper in half like a hamburger. Tape their edges together to form a six-section study guide.

3. This can also be made without using tape by folding the three sheets in half, leaving one side 1" longer than the other.

4. Fold the 1" tab forward over the short side, and then fold it back the other way.

5. Glue the straight edge of each sheet onto the tab of another.

6. As children work through the lessons, have them record math words, concepts, and explanations of subtraction examples.

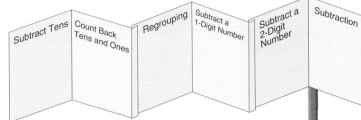

Subtract Tens | Count Back Tens and Ones | Regrouping | Subtract a 1-Digit Number | Subtract a 2-Digit Number | Subtraction

Going Further
Children can use their Accordion Books to review the chapter by comparing their pictures and examples of 2-digit subtraction.

Lesson

1

35 minutes

▶ **Key Strategy**
Use manipulatives

▶ **Format**
Whole class and
student pairs

▶ **Math Vocabulary**
count on, regroup, tens

▶ **Daily Vocabulary**
mental, rewrite, vertical

▶ **Resources**
Learning Resource 19
Teacher Tools 3, 8

Materials
- crayons or colored pencils
- tens and ones models (base-ten set)

Assessment

Check children's mastery of the lesson vocabulary by observing them as they complete the lesson. See page 93 for Assessment Checklist. Remind children to work on their Foldables.

Home Connection

Have children take home their Learning Resource pages to share. Have children show a family member how to add six dimes by skip-counting.

Add Tens and Ones

Math Objective	**ESL/TESOL Descriptors**
■ Add a 1-digit number and a 2-digit number, with and without regrouping.	■ Connect new information to information previously learned. ■ Practice new language.

Activate Prior Knowledge Give pairs Teacher Tool 3: Number Cards. Have pairs order cards from 0 to 100. Repeat, then ask children to skip-count by tens to 100. As they count, write the numbers on a number line. Point out **counting on** by tens can help us mentally add big numbers. Have children count on by **tens** to solve 30 + 20. (*30 + 10 + 10*)

Hands-on Lesson Hand out Teacher Tool 8: Place-Value Workmats and tens and ones models. Write *30 + 20.* Say: *Hold up the number of tens in 30. Put them on your mats. Hold up the number of tens in 20. Put them on your mats. How many tens do you have in all?*

- Point out basic addition facts can also help us add tens. Write and say: *30 + 20 = 3 tens and 2 tens. I know 3 + 2 = 5, so 3 tens + 2 tens = 5 tens. 30 + 20 = 50.* Show how to write the number sentence as a vertical problem.

- Tell children another way to mentally add numbers is to **count on** 1, 2, or 3. Write 26 + 3. Say: *I start at 26 and count on 3 (27, 28, 29). The sum is 29.* Repeat with other 2-digit and 1-digit (1, 2, or 3) numbers.

- Draw a place-value chart. Model this problem: 15 + 7. Say: *I add the ones first. If there are 10 or more one, I regroup.* Draw a circle around 10 ones with an arrow to the tens. Write other 1- and 2-digit problems and have pairs model them. Ask: *Did you need to regroup?* Invite children to give the sum. Hand out Learning Resource 19 for children to complete.

Challenge Have pairs start from 40, and count on by 1, 2, or 3 until they reach 100. Ask children how many 1's, 2's, or 3's they used to reach 100.

Multilevel Strategies

❶ Preproduction
Write *60 + 10 = __*
on the board and invite children to point to the addends and write the sum.

Writing Ask children to write the addition sentence and label the addends and the sum.

❷❸ Early Production and Speech Emergence
Write *60 + 10 = __*
on the board. Ask children to tell you the sum and name the addends.

Writing Ask children to write a sentence with the words *addend* and *sum.*

❹❺ Intermediate and Advanced Fluency
Write *60 + 10 = __*
and ask children to say how they decide if they need to regroup.

Writing Ask children to write the steps for regrouping.

Name _____

Color the Sneakers!

Add the numbers in the number sentences.

When you can count on 1, 2, or 3, color the sneaker

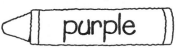

When you can count on by 10's, color the sneaker

When you need to regroup, color the sneaker

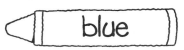

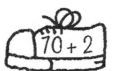

© Macmillan/McGraw-Hill

35 minutes

▶ **Key Strategy**
Use manipulatives

▶ **Format**
Whole class and student pairs

▶ **Math Vocabulary**
addend, regroup

▶ **Daily Vocabulary**
check, different, line up, order, reverse

▶ **Resources**
Learning Resource 20
Teacher Tools 7, 8

Materials
- index cards with 2-digit addition exercises, some requiring regrouping
- tens and ones models (base-ten set)

Assessment

Check children's mastery of the lesson vocabulary by observing them as they complete the lesson. See page 93 for Assessment Checklist. Remind children to work on their Foldables.

Home Connection

Have children take home their Learning Resource pages to share. Ask them to show their family member how to regroup using dimes and pennies.

Add 2-Digit Numbers

Math Objective	**ESL/TESOL Descriptors**
■ Add two 2-digit numbers, with and without regrouping.	■ Use context to construct meaning.
	■ Follow oral and written directions.

Activate Prior Knowledge Write $17 + 4$. Ask a child to model 17 on a place-value mat with tens and ones and then put 4 more ones in the ones place. Ask children to recall what they know about **regrouping**. Ask: ***Do we need to regroup to add 17 + 4? Why?*** *(There are more than 10 ones.)* Then model how to regroup 10 ones as a ten, and add the ones and the tens.

Hands-on Lesson Give pairs tens and ones, and Teacher Tools 7 and 8. Draw a place-value chart and write $27 + 14$ in it. Have pairs use tens and ones to show 27 and 14 on their mats. Model how to add $27 + 14$. Say: ***First we add the ones.*** Ask: ***How many ones are there?*** *(11)* ***Do we need to regroup?*** *(yes)* Model how to regroup 10 ones for a ten.

- Say: ***First I add the ones. There are more than 10, so I regroup 10 ones as a ten. I write 1 above the 2 in the tens place. Then I add the tens. The sum is 41.***

- Give pairs the index cards. One child chooses a card and models the numbers on the place-value mat and the other writes the exercise on the place-value chart. Pairs can work together to find the sum.

- Model how to check addition by reversing the order of the **addends.** Write $53 + 28 = 81$ vertically and say: ***I change the order of the addends to check the sum.*** Write $28 + 53 = $ ___ vertically and add.

- Hand out Learning Resource 20 and read aloud the directions.

Challenge Invite pairs to create word problems using 2-digit numbers. Invite them to exchange their problems with another pair to solve.

Multilevel Strategies

❶ Preproduction
Write $17 + 5$ and $20 + 28$. Point to each and say: ***Nod or say "yes" if we need to regroup.***

Writing Ask children to solve the problems and write *regroup* or *don't regroup.*

❷❸ Early Production and Speech Emergence
Write $17 + 5$ and $20 + 28$. Point to each and ask: ***Do we need to regroup?***

Writing Ask children to solve each problem and write: *I regrouped* or *I did not regroup.*

❹❺ Intermediate and Advanced Fluency
Write $17 + 5$ and $20 + 28$. Ask: ***How do you decide if you need to regroup?***

Writing Ask children to write how they know if they need to regroup.

Name _____

Color the Box!

Add the numbers. If you regroup, color the box.

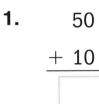

1. 50
    + 10

2. 36
    + 17

3. 40
    + 30

4. 43
    + 23

5. 70
    + 12

6. 55
    + 40

7. 32
    + 23

8. 56
    + 27

9. 48
    + 39

10. 33
    + 35

11. 46
    + 26

12. 27
    + 39

35 minutes

▶ **Key Strategy**
Use manipulatives

▶ **Format**
Whole class and student pairs

▶ **Math Vocabulary**
count back, difference, number sentence, regroup

▶ **Daily Vocabulary**
mental, vertical

▶ **Resources**
Learning Resource 21
Teacher Tools 3, 8

Materials
- crayons or colored pencils
- tens and ones models (base-ten set)

Assessment

Check children's mastery of the lesson vocabulary by observing them as they complete the lesson. See page 93 for Assessment Checklist. Remind children to work on their Foldables.

Home Connection

Have children take home their Learning Resource page to show their family. Ask them to make up two new problems to share.

Subtract Tens and Ones

Math Objective	**ESL/TESOL Descriptors**
▪ Subtract a 1-digit number from a 2-digit number, with and without regrouping.	▪ Use context to construct meaning. ▪ Practice new language.

Activate Prior Knowledge Ask children to **count back** by tens from 100. Make a number line with the numbers. Explain counting back by tens can help us mentally subtract large numbers. Hand out Teacher Tool 3: Number Cards by Tens to pairs. Have them put the cards in order from 100–0.

Hands-on Lesson Hand out tens and ones models and Teacher Tool 8: Place-Value Workmats. Write $70 - 20$. Have children put 7 tens on the mat under the ten. Ask: *How many tens in all?* Have children take away 2 tens and count what is left. Ask: *How many tens do you have now?* Ask children to use the number line to count back 2 tens from 70.

- Say: *Basic facts can also help us subtract. 80 − 30 is the same as 8 tens − 3 tens. I know 8 − 3 = 5, so 8 tens − 3 tens = 5 tens. 80 − 30 = 50.* The **difference** is 50. Show how this **number sentence** can be written vertically.

- Explain another way to subtract some 1-digit numbers from a 2-digit number is to count back. Write $35 - 2$. Say: *I start at 35 and count back 2 (34, 33) so the difference is 33.* Write 2- and 1-digit problems to solve by counting back.

- Draw a place-value chart and model $27 - 8$. Say: *I subtract the ones first. If there are not enough ones, I need to regroup.* Circle a ten and then draw ten more cubes in the ones box. Put an X on the circled ten. Subtract and ask: *How many ones are left?* (9)

- Write more 2-digit and 1-digit problems for children to model on their mats. Hand out Learning Resource 21 for children to complete.

Challenge Have pairs start from 60 and count back by 1, 2, or 3 until they reach 0. Ask how many 1's, 2's, and 3's pairs used to reach 0.

Multilevel Strategies

❶ Preproduction
Write $17 - 5$ and $22 - 8$. Point to each and say: *Nod or say "yes" if we need to regroup.*

Writing Ask children to solve and write *regroup* or *do not regroup* for each.

❷❸ Early Production and Speech Emergence
Write $17 - 5$ and $22 - 8$. Point to each and ask: *Do we need to regroup?*

Writing Ask children to solve and write a sentence about regrouping.

❹❺ Intermediate and Advanced Fluency
Ask: *How do we know when we need to regroup?*

Writing Ask children to write the steps for regrouping.

Name _____

Color the Wheels!

Subtract.

If you count back 1, 2, or 3, color the skates red.

If you count back by 10s, color the skates yellow.

When you need to regroup, color the skates orange.

13
−3

60
−2

77
−3

50
−10

40
−20

72
−9

52
−4

21
−8

43
−3

▶ **Key Strategy**
Use manipulatives

▶ **Format**
Whole class and student pairs

▶ **Math Vocabulary**
addend, difference, inverse regroup

▶ **Daily Vocabulary**
check

▶ **Resources**
Learning Resource 22
Teacher Tools 7, 8

Materials

- index cards with 2-digit subtraction problems, some requiring regrouping
- tens and ones models (base-ten set)

Assessment

Check children's mastery of the lesson vocabulary by observing them as they complete the lesson. See page 93 for Assessment Checklist.
Remind children to work on their Foldables.

Home Connection

Have children take home their Learning Resource page to share. Ask them to show their family how to regroup with

Subtract 2-Digit Numbers

Math Objectives	**ESL/TESOL Descriptors**
■ Subtract 2-digit numbers, with and without regrouping.	■ Use context to construct meaning. ■ Follow oral and written directions.

Activate Prior Knowledge Write *24 − 8*. Model 24 on a place-value mat with tens and ones, then put 8 more ones under the 4 in the ones place. Ask children to recall what they know about **regrouping**. Ask: ***Do we need to regroup to subtract 8 from 24? Why?*** *(There are not enough ones.)* Then model how to regroup 10 as ten ones and subtract the ones and then the tens.

Hands-on Lesson Give pairs tens and ones, and Teacher Tools 7 and 8. Draw a place-value chart with *34 − 15* in it. Have pairs show 34 and 15 on their mats. Model how to subtract. Say: ***First we subtract the ones. Are there enough ones to subtract 5? Do we need to regroup?*** Model how to regroup 1 ten as 10 ones.

- Model the exercise again. Say: ***First I subtract the ones. There are not enough ones, so I regroup 1 ten as 10 ones. I cross out the 3 and write a 2. Then I cross out the 4 and write a 14. Then I can subtract to find the difference.*** *(19)*

- Give pairs the index cards. One child chooses a card and models the numbers on the place-value mat while the other writes the exercise on a place-value chart. Pairs can work together to find the differences.

- Model how to check subtraction by using the inverse operation. Write *35 − 15 = 19* vertically and say: ***I can use addition to check subtraction.*** Write *19 + 15 = 34*. Point how how the **addends** are reversed.

- Distribute Learning Resource 22 and have children complete the page.

Challenge Invite pairs to create word problems using 2-digit numbers. Invite them to exchange problems with another pair to solve.

Multilevel Strategies

1 Preproduction
Write *28 − 15* and *62 − 54*. Point to each and say: ***Nod or say yes if we need to regroup.***

Writing Ask children to solve the problems and write *regroup* or *don't regroup*.

2 3 Early Production and Speech Emergence
Write *28 − 15* and *62 − 54*. Point to each and ask: ***Do we need to regroup?***

Writing Ask children to solve each problem and write: *I regrouped* or *I did not regroup.*

4 5 Intermediate and Advanced Fluency
Write *28 − 15* and *62 − 54*. Ask: ***How do you know when to regroup?***

Writing Ask children to write how they know if they need to regroup.

Name _____

Color the Squares!

Subtract.

Color the squares when you need to regroup.

1.   36
    − 25
    ☐

2.   70
    − 29
    ☐

3.   26
    − 12
    ☐

4.   56
    − 27
    ☐

5.   68
    − 33
    ☐

6.   43
    − 14
    ☐

7.   90
    − 35
    ☐

8.   54
    − 13
    ☐

9.   80
    − 26
    ☐

10.   77
    − 10
    ☐

11.   25
    − 16
    ☐

12.   87
    − 35
    ☐

Lesson 5

 35 minutes

▶ **Key Strategy**
Use visuals

▶ **Format**
Whole class, groups,
student pairs

▶ **Math Vocabulary**
estimate, reasonable, round
down, round up

▶ **Daily Vocabulary**
less, more, nearer, nearest

▶ **Resources**
Learning Resource 23

Materials
- butcher paper for
  number lines
- index cards
- markers

Assessment

Check children's mastery of the
lesson vocabulary by observing
them as they complete the
lesson. See page 93 for
Assessment Checklist.
Remind children to work on their
Foldables.

Home Connection

Have children take home their
Learning Resource page and
work with a family member to
write a new problem to share.

Estimate Sums and Differences

Math Objectives	**ESL/TESOL Descriptors**
■ Estimate sums.	■ Participate in full class, group, and pair discussions.
■ Estimate differences.	■ Use context to construct meaning.

Activate Prior Knowledge Draw a number line from 30–50. Circle 37. Ask: *Is 37 nearer to 40 or to 30?* Repeat with other numbers. Ask each child to circle a number and ask classmates a "nearer to" question.

Hands-on Lesson Say: *When we round a number to the nearest 10, we call it the number that is the nearest multiple of 10. For example, we round 37 to 40 since 37 is nearer 40 than 30.* Draw a number line from 0–10. Put an X on 5. Say: *When we round, we look at the number in the ones place. If the number is 4 or less, we* round down *to the nearest 10. If the number is 5 or greater, we* round up.

- Write *49 + 32* vertically. Point to 49 and ask: *Do we round up to 50 or round down to 40? Why?* Write *50* next to 49. Point to 32 and ask: *Do we round up to 40 or round down to 30? Why?* Write *30* next to 32. Say: *We can round to quickly* estimate *the sum since it is easier to add 50 + 30 = 80.* Add both problems and compare the sums. Ask: *Was the estimate* reasonable?

- Write *37 − 25* vertically and repeat the steps described above to have children estimate the difference.

- Have pairs write 5 numbers from 10 to 30 on index cards. One child takes two cards from the pile, rounds the numbers to the nearest ten, and estimates the sum. The other estimates the difference between the two numbers. Then they solve the problems without rounding to decide if the estimate was reasonable.

- Hand out Learning Resource 23 for children to complete.

Challenge Have groups draw a number line for 20 numbers, such as 40–60. Ask them to create problems and estimate the answers by rounding.

Multilevel Strategies

1 Preproduction
Say a number and invite children to point to the nearest multiple of ten on the number line.

Writing Ask children to write the number and round it up or down to the nearest ten.

2 3 Early Production and Speech Emergence
Say a number and ask children if you need to round up or down to the nearest ten.

Writing Ask children to write the new number and *I round up* or *I round down*.

4 5 Intermediate and Advanced Fluency
Say a number and ask children to explain how to round it to the nearest ten.

Writing Ask children to write how they know whether to round up or down.

Name _____

Rounding Numbers

Round the numbers to the nearest 10. Then add or subtract.

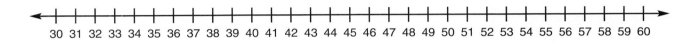

1. $\quad 46 \rightarrow$ ____
$\quad - 41 \rightarrow -$____

2. $\quad 45 \rightarrow$ ____
$\quad - 31 \rightarrow -$____

3. $\quad 45 \rightarrow$ ____
$\quad + 44 \rightarrow -$____

4. $\quad 54 \rightarrow$ ____
$\quad - 41 \rightarrow -$____

5. $\quad 57 \rightarrow$ ____
$\quad - 43 \rightarrow -$____

6. $\quad 23 \rightarrow$ ____
$\quad + 39 \rightarrow -$____

7. $\quad 31 \rightarrow$ ____
$\quad + 15 \rightarrow -$____

8. $\quad 54 \rightarrow$ ____
$\quad - 31 \rightarrow -$____

9. $\quad 14 \rightarrow$ ____
$\quad + 34 \rightarrow -$____

10. $\quad 16 \rightarrow$ ____
$\quad + 13 \rightarrow -$____

11. $\quad 45 \rightarrow$ ____
$\quad - 32 \rightarrow -$____

12. $\quad 19 \rightarrow$ ____
$\quad + 11 \rightarrow -$____

Lesson 6

35 minutes

▶ **Key Strategy**
Use visuals

▶ **Format**
Whole class and student pairs

▶ **Math Vocabulary**
addend, double, sum

▶ **Daily Vocabulary**
strategy

▶ **Resources**
Learning Resource 24

Materials
• index cards with 2-digit numbers

Assessment

Check children's mastery of the lesson vocabulary by observing them as they complete the lesson. See page 93 for Assessment Checklist. Remind children to work on their Foldables.

Home Connection

Have children take home their Learning Resource page and work with a family member to make a new problem to share.

Add Three Addends

Math Objective	ESL/TESOL Descriptors
■ Add three 2-digit numbers.	■ Select, connect, and explain information. ■ Practice new language.

Activate Prior Knowledge Ask children to recall the strategies they know for adding. *(make a ten, add doubles, counting on)* Explain that we can use some of these strategies to add three **addends.** Write *6 + 4 + 3.* Ask: ***What strategy can we use to add these numbers?*** Elicit from children that they could make a ten and then add three. Write *make a ten* and ask a child to circle the two numbers that make a ten. Write *4 + 4 + 7.* Ask: ***What strategy can we use to add these numbers?*** Elicit from children they could add the **doubles** first. Write *add doubles* and ask a child to circle the doubles.

Hands-on Lesson Write *12 + 13 + 27* vertically. Ask: ***What numbers do you see in the ones column that might help you make a ten or a double?*** Circle 3 and 7 and write 10 next to the problem. Ask a child to find the **sum.**

• Hand out index cards with a 2-digit numbers. Have pairs take turns to choose three cards, look for a strategy, and name the strategy. Encourage children to say: ***I can make a ten or I can add doubles.*** The child writes the numbers vertically on a piece of paper, circles the strategy numbers and adds.

• When pairs have finished, invite volunteers to show their problems and explain the strategy they used to add each one. Hand out Learning Resource 24: Smart Strategies for children to complete.

Challenge Write *45 + 15 + 15 + 10.* Ask children to use the strategies they know to add four numbers. Invite pairs to create their own problems with four numbers which can be solved by "make a ten" or "add doubles."

Multilevel Strategies

1 Preproduction
Write *12 + 17 + 12* and say: ***Draw a circle around the numbers that make adding three numbers easier.***

Writing Ask children to copy the name of the strategy from the board.

2 3 Early Production and Speech Emergence
Write *12 + 17 + 12.* Ask: ***What strategy can we use to solve this problem?***

Writing Ask children to write the name of the strategy.

4 5 Intermediate and Advanced Fluency
Write *12 + 17 + 12.* Ask children to explain a strategy they can use to add the numbers.

Writing Ask children to explain the other strategy that makes it easier to add three numbers.

Name _____

Smart Strategies!

Choose three numbers from the number box.

Write the numbers and add them. Use "make a ten" and "add doubles" as often as you can. Name the strategy you use. The first one is done for you.

45 25 28 1 3 5 2 9 8 22 16 32
10 14 19 26 33 17 1 4 24 11

1.
```
    4 5
    1 1
  + 2 5
  -----
    8 1
```
Strategy: Make 10

2.
```
    ___
    ___
  + ___
  -----
    ___
```
Strategy: _____

3.
```
    ___
    ___
  + ___
  -----
    ___
```
Strategy: Make 10

4.
```
    ___
    ___
  + ___
  -----
    ___
```
Strategy: _____

5.
```
    ___
    ___
  + ___
  -----
    ___
```
Strategy: Make 10

6.
```
    ___
    ___
  + ___
  -----
    ___
```
Strategy: _____

© Macmillan/McGraw-Hill

Problem Solving
Reading for Math

SKILL: Draw a Pattern

Model the skill using a word problem such as the following:

1 Leona has a box of bright beads. She wants to make a necklace. 15 beads are blue, 12 beads are yellow, and 3 beads are green. How can she make a pattern with the beads using every one?

2 I can use connecting cubes to make a pattern. Then I can draw the pattern for the necklace.

3 I can carry out my plan.
I can draw my pattern.

4 I can check my pattern to see if it uses all of the beads. I can check to see if the pattern repeats. I can see how many times the pattern repeats.

Distribute **Math Center Card 4A** to children.

Math Center Card 4A

Reading for Math Skill

PROBLEMS AND SOLUTIONS • DRAW A PATTERN

You need: red, yellow, blue, and green counters (4 of each color), drawing paper, crayons

1. Read the story.
   Amos the clown loves buttons.
   He wants to put a row of buttons down his shirt.
   He has 4 red buttons, 4 yellow buttons, and 4 blue buttons.
   Help Amos make a pattern.

2. Use counters to show a pattern for Amos's 12 buttons.

3. Draw a large picture of the clown's shirt. Color the pattern of buttons.

Math Center Card, Grade 2, Unit 4, 4A

STRATEGY: Choose the Operation

Model the strategy using a word problem such as the following:

Read Kim and Farouk bought prizes for the fair. Kim bought 17 prizes. Farouk bought 6 prizes. How many more did Kim buy?

Plan **Think:** What do I already know?
Kim bought 17 prizes.
Farouk bought 6 prizes.
I can subtract to find the difference.

Solve I can carry out my plan.

$$
\begin{array}{r}
17 \\
-6 \\
\hline
11
\end{array}
$$

Kim bought 11 more prizes than Farouk.

Look Back I'll check my answer by adding.
$11 + 6 = 17$
Does my answer make sense?
Yes.

Distribute **Math Center Card 4B** to children.

Math Center Card 4B

Problem Solving: Strategy

CHOOSE THE OPERATION • NUMBERS AND QUESTIONS

You need: 10 cards, 4 strips of paper

1. Write a number on each card. Pick numbers between 10 and 90.
   32 17 79

2. Write these questions on strips of paper. Write a different question on each paper.
   How many are there now?   How many are there in all?
   How many are left?   How many more ___ are there than ___?

3. Take turns picking 2 numbers and 1 question. Use them to write a number story. You can write about animals, plants, toys, or anything you want.
   There are dogs and birds at the pet store.
   There are 17 dogs and 32 birds.
   How many more birds are there than dogs?

4. Trade stories with your partner. Solve. Write a number sentence.

5. Check each other's answers.

Math Center Card, Grade 2, Unit 4, 4B

Assessment Checklist

	STUDENT NAMES										
SCHOOL:											
TEACHER:　　　　**SCHOOL YEAR:**											
Mark: + = Mastery √ = Satisfactory – = Needs Improvement											
LEVEL OF LANGUAGE PROFICIENCY (1–5)											
MATH OBJECTIVES											
• Add a 1-digit number and a 2-digit number.											
• Add two 2-digit numbers, with and without regrouping.											
• Add three 2-digit numbers.											
• Subtract a 1-digit number from a 2-digit number.											
• Subtract two 2-digit numbers, with and without regrouping.											
ESL/TESOL LISTENING/SPEAKING											
Demonstrate knowledge through application in a variety of contexts.											
Follow oral and written directions.											
Listen to and imitate how others use English.											
Practice new language.											
Select, connect, and explain information.											
Use context to construct meaning.											
ESL/TESOL READING											
Apply basic reading comprehension skills.											
Use context to construct meaning.											
Listen to, speak and read about subject matter information.											
ESL WRITING											
Write to demonstrate comprehension.											
Write using spelling patterns and targeted English vocabulary.											

Foldables

1 Preproduction
- Did students write the unit vocabulary?
- Did they copy the definitions?

2 3 Early Production and Speech Emergence
- Did students label the tabs correctly?
- Did they write the vocabulary words?
- Did they copy the definitions?

4 5 Intermediate and Advanced Fluency
- Did students write definitions for the unit vocabulary?
- Did they use correct spelling and grammar?

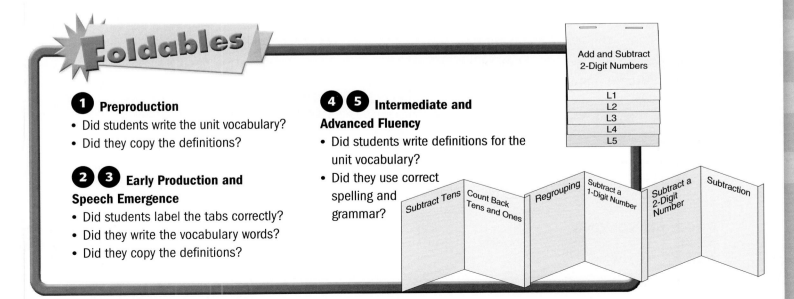

UNIT 5

Planner

Measurement and Geometry

Assessment
p. 115
• Assessment Checklist
• Foldables

LOG ON Visit **www.mmhmath.com**

Unit Activities	• **Activity 1** Readiness Make a Geoperson, p. 98	• **Activity 3** Compare to a Kilogram, p. 99
	• **Activity 2** Snail Perimeters, p. 98	• **Activity 4** Pattern Block Symmetry, p. 99

Lessons	Key Objectives	Vocabulary	Materials	Resources
READ TOGETHER "Shapes" by Sandra Liastos, pp. 96–97	**Math:** Identify 2-dimensional shapes and their attributes. **ESL/TESOL:** Goal 1, Standard 3.	angle, circle, computer, everywhere, frames, shape, size, square, triangle		Graphic Organizer 3 **Overhead Manipulatives**
UNIT WARM-UP Understanding Measurement p. 100	**Math:** Estimate and measure length. **ESL/TESOL:** Goal 1/3, Standard 3/3.	estimate, length, longer, measure, shorter, unit	crayons, cubes, paper clips, yarn or string	**Overhead Manipulatives**
LESSON 1 Measure Length pp. 102–103	**Math:** Measure length in customary and metric units. **ESL/TESOL:** Goal 2, Standard 3.	centimeter (cm), distance, foot, inch (in.), meter (m), yard	butcher paper, crayons or markers, tape, yardstick, yarn	Learning Resource 25
LESSON 2 Measure Capacity pp. 104–105	**Math:** Measure capacity in customary and metric units. **ESL/TESOL:** Goal 2, Standard 1.	capacity, cup (c), fluid ounce (fl oz), gallon (gal), liter (l), milliliter (ml), pint (p), quart (qt)	beans, containers, medicine cup, measuring tools	Learning Resource 26
LESSON 3 Weight and Mass pp. 106–107	**Math:** Measure weight in customary and metric units. **ESL/TESOL:** Goal 2, Standard 3.	gram (g), kilogram (kg), mass, ounce (oz), pound (lb)	balance scale, paper clip, plastic jar of beans, weights	Learning Resource 27
LESSON 4 Measure Temperature pp. 108–109	**Math:** Read temperatures. **ESL/TESOL:** Goal 1, Standard 3.	degrees Celsius (°C), degrees Fahrenheit (°F), temperature	thermometers, glue, markers, old magazines, scissors	Learning Resource 28 Teacher Tool 20
LESSON 5 2- and 3-Dimensional Figures pp. 110–111	**Math:** Identify 2- and 3-dimensional figures and their attributes. **ESL/TESOL:** Goal 2, Standard 3.	angle, circle, cone, cube, cylinder, edge, face, hexagon, parallelogram, etc.	multicolored squares, pattern blocks, sets of shapes	Learning Resource 29
LESSON 6 Spatial Concepts pp. 112–113	**Math:** Identify congruence and symmetry; slides, flips, and turns. Find perimeter and area. **ESL/TESOL:** Goal 1, Standard 3.	area, congruent, flip, line of symmetry, perimeter, slide, turn	index cards, pattern blocks, premade paper shapes	Teacher Tool 9 and 11
PROBLEM SOLVING p. 114 • Skill: Use Illustrations • Strategy: Guess and Check	Use skills and strategies to solve problems.			**Math Center Cards 5A, 5B**

Math at Home

See **Math at Home Family Guide** for additional math vocabulary, activities, and games in English, Spanish, and Haitian Creole.

© Macmillan/McGraw-Hill

English Vocabulary

Dear Family: *Please help your child practice the key vocabulary words for this unit.*

area the size of a surface that is inside a boundary or perimeter; area is measured in square units

degrees Celsius a unit of measure of temperature in the metric system ($^\circ$C)

degrees Fahrenheit a unit of measure of temperature in degrees ($^\circ$F)

edge the line on a solid shape where two surfaces meet

face a flat surface of a solid shape

length tells how long something is

perimeter the distance around a shape

side the edge of a 2-dimensional figure

symmetry the feature of having two identical halves

Vocabulario en español

Estimados familiares: *Por favor ayuden a su hijo/a a practicar las palabras del vocabulario de esta unidad.*

área el tamaño de una superficie dentro de un límite o perímetro; el área se mide en unidades cuadradas

grados Celsius unidad para medir la temperatura en el sistema métrico ($^\circ$C)

grados Fahrenheit unidad para medir la temperatura en grados ($^\circ$F)

arista la línea de una figura sólida donde se unen dos superficies

cara superficie plana de una figura sólida

longitud indica el largo de algo

perímetro la distancia alrededor de una figura

lado la línea de una figura bidimensional

simetría la característica de tener dos mitades idénticas

Vokabilè an kreyol

Chè paran: *Tanpri ede pitit la pratike mo vokabilè nan seksyon sa a.*

sifas se dimansyon ki andedan yon perimèt; yo mezire è an inite kare

degre Celsius se yon inite ki itilize pou mezire tanperati an degre ($^\circ$C) nan sistèm metrik la

degre Fahrenheit se yon inite ki itilize pou mezire tanperati an degre ($^\circ$F)

bòdi se lign ki nan yon figi a twa dimansyon kote 2 sifas rankontre

fas se yon sifas plat ki nan yon fòm a 3 dimansyon

lomgè sa diw ki longè on bagay ye

perimèt se distans ki nan alantou yon figi

kote se lizyè yon figi a 2 dimansyon

simetri se an bagay pou gen 2 mwatye ki sanble tèt koupe

SHAPES

by Sandra Liastos

 30 minutes

Math Objective
- Identify 2-dimensional shapes and their attributes.

ESL/TESOL Descriptors
- Listen to and imitate how others use English.
- Select, connect, and explain information.

Reading Skills
- Summarize

Vocabulary
angle, benches, breeze, bubbles, circle, clouds, computer, everywhere, fences, frames, pies, robots, shape, size, square, triangle

Before Reading

Build Background/Oral Language
Hold up a triangle, circle, and square one at a time and ask children to find each shape in the classroom. Show examples of angles and ask children to find angles. You may want to use Attribute Blocks from **Overhead Manipulatives.** Explain that you will read a poem about shapes and angles.

During Reading

- Read the poem through as children listen. Invite them to ask about any difficult or new words.
- Read the poem line by line. Invite children to repeat each line after you.
- Divide the class into four groups and ask each group to read one line of each verse. (If there are more than four lines, all read the last line together.)

Phonological/Phonemic Awareness
Draw attention to the rhyming pattern in the poem by rereading the lines that rhyme. Encourage children to underline the rhyming words.

After Reading

- Help children summarize the poem. Ask: *What are some shapes in the poem? Where are the shapes? What is the poet telling us?*
- Ask children to put these headings in their 4-column chart: *angles, triangles, circles,* and *squares.* Ask children to write where the different places the poet sees each shape. Encourage them to add some of their own.

Art Invite children to make geometric pictures using cutout triangles, circles, and squares.

Assessment

Observe children's participation as they read the poem. See Assessment Checklist on page 115.

Multilevel Strategies

1 **Preproduction**
Hold up a square and ask: *Can you find a square in the classroom?* Ask children to touch or point to the square. Repeat with circle, triangle, and angle.

Writing Draw, write, and say the names of various shapes and ask children to copy them.

2 **3** **Early Production and Speech Emergence**
Point to shapes in the classroom and ask: *What is this shape?*

Writing Draw various shapes and ask children to write the names.

4 **5** **Intermediate and Advanced Fluency**
Say: *Can you think of some things that have a square shape?* Encourage them to name as many as they can. Repeat with circle.

Writing Challenge children to write the names of as many things as they can that have a triangle shape.

SHAPES

by Sandra Liatsos

Angle,
  Triangle,
Circle,
  Square,
Shapes of all sizes
  Are everywhere;

Angles in elbows,
  Angles in fences,
Angles in clouds,
  And hard, park benches.

Circles in bubbles,
  Circles in pies,
Circles in faces,
  And in your eyes.

Squares in computers
  And picture frames,
Squares in robots,
  And boards for games.

We've triangle hats,
  And triangle trees,
And triangle sails
  Holding a breeze.

Angle
  Triangle,
Circle,
  Square,
Shapes of all sizes
  Are everywhere!

Activities

Activities

Readiness
ACTIVITY 1

INDIVIDUAL

Make a Geoperson

YOU NEED
Clay

- Head: a cube

- Body: a rectangular prism

- Eyes: spheres

- Ears: cones

- Arms and legs: cylinders

Identify 3-Dimensional Figures

© Macmillan/McGraw-Hill

ACTIVITY 2

PARTNERS

Snail Perimeters

YOU NEED
centimeter ruler
calculator

The snail crawls around the edge of each shape. How far does it go?

- Trace shape A. Measure each side with a centimeter ruler. Add the measurements of all of the sides. Use a calculator. Write: "The perimeter is _____ ." Check your partner's answer.

- Do the same steps for the other shapes.

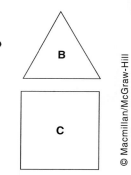

© Macmillan/McGraw-Hill

See answers on page 193.

Find the Perimeters of Shapes

Game Zone

ACTIVITY 3

PARTNERS

Compared to a Kilogram

Choose an object in the classroom. Hold the object.

YOU NEED

- Estimate if the object weighs more or less than 1 kilogram.

- Weigh the object. If your estimate was right, you get one point.

- The player with the most points after five turns wins.

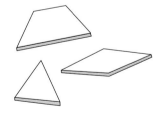

Measure Weight in Metric Units

ACTIVITY 4

PARTNERS

Pattern Block Symmetry

Take turns. Use pattern blocks.

YOU NEED

pattern blocks

- Draw a line. This is a line of symmetry.

- Choose a block. Put it over the middle of the line of symmetry.

- Trace the part of the block on one side of the line of symmetry. Your partner traces the matching part.

- Next, make a pattern. Draw it on one side of the line.

- Your partner draws the same pattern on the other side of the line.

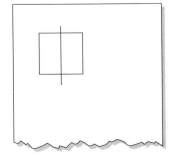

Identify Symmetrical Shapes

© Macmillan/McGraw-Hill

Warm-Up

 30 minutes

▶ **Key Strategy**
Use manipulatives

▶ **Format**
Whole class and small groups

▶ **Math Vocabulary**
length, measure, unit

▶ **Daily Vocabulary**
estimate, longer, shorter

▶ **Resource**
Overhead Manipulatives:
Connecting Cubes

▶ **Materials**
crayons, cubes, paper clips, yarn or string (2 colors)

LOG ON Visit **www.mmhmath.com** to find printable **Vocabulary Cards** that help build academic language.

Understanding Measurement

Math Objective	ESL/TESOL Descriptors
■ Estimate and measure length.	■ Use context to construct meaning.
	■ Observe and model how others speak in a particular situation.

Activate Prior Knowledge Put some crayons of different lengths on a table. Hold up two crayons and say: *These crayons are different lengths.* Ask: *Which is longer?* Hold up two different crayons and ask: *Which is shorter?* Invite children to take turns choosing two crayons and saying: *This crayon is longer* or *This crayon is shorter.*

Hands-on Lesson Put a pile of connecting cubes and paper clips on a table, along with various classroom objects that are different lengths. Model for children how to use cubes and paper clips to **estimate** and **measure** the **lengths** of different objects. You may wish to use the Connecting Cubes from **Overhead Manipulatives.**

● Display a marker. Say: *I can measure the length of this marker with cubes.* Hold up a cube. Ask: *How many cubes long do you think this marker is? What is your estimate?* Write the children's estimate on the board.

● Model how to measure length by aligning the first cube with the end of the marker, and then continue to place the cubes side by side until the cubes reach the end of the marker. Ask: *What is the length of this marker in cubes?* Count the number of cubes in unison. (Point out that the measurement will not be exact.)

● Hold up a paper clip and invite a volunteer to estimate the length of the marker in paper clips. Ask: *What is the length of the marker in paper clips?*

● Invite children to work in groups to estimate, measure, and record the lengths of classroom objects using paper clips and cubes. Ask early finishers to try measuring greater lengths with different units of measurement, such as a foot.

Multilevel Strategies

❶ Preproduction
Hold up two different colored pieces of yarn. Say: *Point to the yarn that is shorter.* Hold up two different pieces. Say: *Point to the yarn that is longer.*

❷❸ Early Production and Speech Emergence
Hold up two different colored pieces of yarn. Ask children to say which yarn is shorter by naming its color (or pointing) and saying: *It is shorter.*

❹❺ Intermediate and Advanced Fluency
Put pieces of yarn on a table and ask children to work with a partner, taking turns asking *What is the length?* and measuring it with cubes.

Procedure: Help children make these Foldables to write vocabulary words and definitions throughout the unit. Encourage children to use the Foldables as a study guide.

Layered-Look Book

1. Provide each child with three sheets of 11" × 17" paper, or use three 6-foot-long sheets of bulletin-board paper to make one large classroom Layered-Look Book.

2. Place the sheets of paper an equal distance apart as illustrated.

3. Roll the bottom of the three sheets up to make five tabs the same size. Fold, glue, and staple.

4. Have children write math words, definitions, symbols, and examples under the tabs.

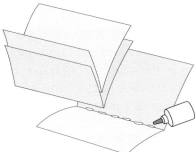

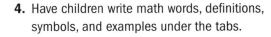

Spatial Sense
Congruence
Symmetry
Slides, Flips, and Turns
Perimeter
Area

Going Further
Children can use their Layered-Look Books to review by comparing their pictures and examples of congruence, symmetry, perimeter, area, and rotations.

Accordion Book

1. Provide each child with three sheets of 11" × 17" paper.

2. Fold the sheets in half like hamburgers. Tape their edges together to form a six-section study guide.

3. You can also make this without using tape by folding the three sheets in half and leaving one side 1" longer than the other.

4. Fold the 1" tab forward over the short side, then fold it back the other way.

5. Glue the straight edge sheet onto the tab of another.

6. As children work through the lessons, have them record math words, definitions, and information on measurement and geometry.

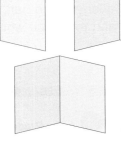

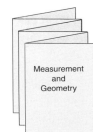

Measurement and Geometry

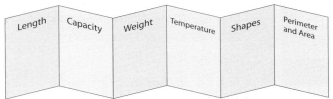

Length Capacity Weight Temperature Shapes Perimeter and Area

Going Further
Children can use their Accordion Books to review by comparing their pictures and examples of measurement and geometry.

 45 minutes

▶ **Key Strategy**
Use manipulatives

▶ **Format**
Whole class and small groups

▶ **Math Vocabulary**
centimeter (cm), distance, foot, inch (in.), meter (m), yard

▶ **Daily Vocabulary**
customary, height, long, metric, wide, yardstick

▶ **Resources**
Learning Resource 25

Materials
- butcher paper
- crayons or markers
- inch ruler
- yardstick
- meter stick
- yarn

Assessment

Check children's mastery of the lesson vocabulary by observing them while measuring different objects. See Assessment Checklist on page 115.

Home Connection

Have children take home their Learning Resource pages to share. Encourage them to show a family member how to measure the length of an object using pennies.

Measure Length

Math Objective	**ESL/TESOL Descriptors**
▪ Measure length in customary and metric units.	▪ Connect new information to information previously learned. ▪ Demonstrate knowledge through application.

Activate Prior Knowledge Have each child trace their foot and cut out the tracing. Then hand out large and small paper clips. Ask children to estimate the length of their feet in big paper clips, then measure. Repeat with small paper clips. Discuss the accuracy of the estimates. Ask: *Why do you need more of the smaller paper clips to measure your foot? (Smaller clips cover shorter lengths.)*

Hands-on Activity Display an **inch** ruler, yardstick, **centimeter** ruler, and **meter** stick. Discuss how we use these units to find length—the **distance** between two points. Make a display chart that shows 12 inches = 1 foot and 3 **feet** = 1 **yard**.

- Ask two children to measure the length of the board with an inch ruler and a yardstick. Ask: *Which is the best unit for measuring it? (yardstick) Why? (because it is a larger unit of measure)* Point out that it is important to know which unit to use when measuring. Have children estimate and measure classroom items, e.g., paintbrushes, books, desks, distance from desk to door, etc.

- Tape an 8-cm piece of yarn on the board. Display a centimeter ruler and meter stick. Discuss how we can also use these metric **units of measure** to find length. Ask: *Which is the best unit for measuring the yarn? (centimeter ruler) Why? (because it is a smaller unit of measure)* Record the children's estimate of the length of the yarn, then measure. Then invite children to measure classroom objects again.

- Help children complete Learning Resource 25: Measuring Fun.

Challenge Ask pairs to find the length of a hall, using footprints, inches, centimeters, yards, and meters, and to decide which unit was best.

Multilevel Strategies

1 Preproduction
Name different measuring tools and have children point to them.

Writing Write the names of different measuring tools for children to copy.

2 3 Early Production and Speech Emergence
Hold up a measuring tool and ask: *What can I measure with this (inch ruler)?*

Writing Ask children to measure the objects and write the results.

4 5 Intermediate and Advanced Fluency
Ask children to explain how to measure the length of an object.

Writing Ask children to write names of measurement tools and the items they measured.

Name _____

Measuring Fun

Estimate the length.

Then use a 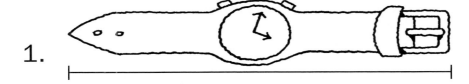 to measure.

1.

Estimate: about _____ in. Measure: about _____ in.

2.

Estimate: about _____ in. Measure: about _____ in.

Estimate the length.

Then use a  to measure.

3.

Estimate: about _____ cm Measure: about _____ cm

© Macmillan/McGraw-Hill

Lesson 2

 45 minutes

▶ **Key Strategy**
Use visuals

▶ **Format**
Whole class and student pairs

▶ **Math Vocabulary**
capacity, cup (c), fluid ounce (fl oz), gallon (gal), half gallon, liter (l), milliliter (ml), pint (p), quart (qt)

▶ **Daily Vocabulary**
about the same as, less than, more than

▶ **Resource**
Learning Resource 26

Materials
• empty containers (including pint, quart, gallon, liter)
• 1 milliliter measure
• measuring cup
• water

Assessment

Check children's mastery of the lesson vocabulary by observing them while exploring capacity. See Assessment Checklist on page 115.

Home Connection

Families can estimate the capacity in cups of different containers and then checking the measure with water.

Measure Capacity

Math Objective	**ESL/TESOL Descriptors**
■ Measure capacity in customary and metric units.	■ Follow oral and written directions. ■ Use context to construct meaning.

Activate Prior Knowledge Hold up two liquid containers. Ask: **Which container holds more? Why?** Elicit that the larger the container, the more it will hold. Hold up two more containers. Ask: **Which container holds less? Why?** *(The smaller the container, the less it will hold.)* Invite volunteers to put the containers in order, from biggest to smallest capacity.

Hands-on Lesson Identify the **cup, quart, pint, half gallon** and **gallon** measures. Explain these are units of **capacity**. Write: *How many **fluid ounces** are in a cup? How many cups in a pint? How many pints in a quart? How many quarts in a gallon?*

• Display a **liter** measure. Discuss that this is also a unit of capacity. Show children a **milliliter** measure. Point out that we can use the milliliter to measure small amounts, such as medicine.

• Distribute Learning Resource 26: The Water Test and give each group a set of measuring tools. Ask students to use water to answer questions 1 and 2. (*1 pint = 2 cups; 1 quart = 4 cups; 1 quart = 2 pints; 1 gallon = 8 pints*) Then have them measure and compare the units in questions 3 and 4. Model comparative sentences. *(A half gallon holds more than a liter.)*

Challenge Play an estimation game. Provide quart and gallon containers and a small plastic container of unknown capacity. Children estimate how many small containers they need to fill the quart and gallon, and then measure with water.

Multilevel Strategies

1 Preproduction
Say: **Show me (one quart).** Have children show the measured amount of water.

Writing Write the names of the measuring units and ask children to copy them.

2 3 Early Production and Speech Emergence
Ask: **How many cups are in a quart?** *(four cups)*

Writing Ask children to write the names of the measuring units.

4 5 Intermediate and Advanced Fluency
Ask children to describe how cups, pints, quarts, and gallons are related. *(There are 4 cups in a quart.)*

Writing Ask children to write sentences that tell how cups, pints, quarts and gallons are related.

Name _____

The Water Test!

Use a 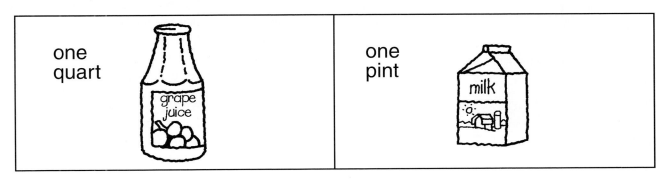 and water to find the answers.

1. Number of cups in	2. Number of pints in
_____ - - - - 1 pint: _____	_____ - - - - 1 quart: _____
_____ - - - - 1 quart: _____	_____ - - - - 1 gallon: _____

3. Which holds more?

one half gallon	1 liter

4. Which holds less?

one quart	one pint

 45 minutes

▶ **Key Strategy**
Use visuals

▶ **Format**
Whole class and small groups

▶ **Math Vocabulary**
gram (g), kilogram (kg), mass, ounce (oz), pound (lb)

▶ **Daily Vocabulary**
heaviest, less than, more than, lightest, weigh, weight

▶ **Resource**
Learning Resource 27

Materials
- balance scale
- classroom objects
- paper clip
- plastic jar of beans
- weights: oz, lb, g, kg

Assessment

Check children's mastery of the lesson vocabulary by observing them decide the approximate weight of an object. See Assessment Checklist on page 101.
Remind children to work on their Foldables.

Home Connection

Ask children to work with a family member to estimate the weight of different objects and then weigh them. Ask them to share the results with the class.

Weight and Mass

Math Objective	**ESL/TESOL Descriptors**
■ Measure weight in customary and metric units.	■ Use context to construct meaning. ■ Negotiate and manage interaction to accomplish tasks.

Activate Prior Knowledge Pass around small classroom objects. Ask: *Which object weighs the most? Which object weighs the least?* Allow children to hold the items again before they make a choice. Then ask children to rank the objects from heaviest to lightest.

Hands-on Lesson Display a 1-ounce weight or object and a jar of beans weighing approximately 1 pound. Explain that we often measure weight in **ounces** or **pounds.** Give each child a chance to hold each object.

- Display a big box of crayons, a marker, a toy ball, and a bag of 20 pennies. Hold up a marker and ask: *Which weighs more—the marker or the jar of beans?* Ask a child to hold both objects, give an answer, and then use the balance scale to check. Continue the activity with other objects.

- Display a 1-**gram** weight or object and a 1-**kilogram** weight or object. Say: *Sometimes people measure weight in* **grams or kilograms.** Give each child a chance to hold each object.

- Display a big jar of paint, a toy animal, a cube, and a bag of 10 counters. Ask: *Which weighs more—the jar of paint or the gram weight?* Ask a child to hold the objects, give an answer, and then use the balance to check. Continue this activity with other objects. Hand out Learning Resource 27 for children to complete.

Challenge Assign four groups one of the following units: ounce, pound, gram, kilogram. Invite children to go on a scavenger hunt for objects that are about the same weight as their assigned unit. Ask them to make a list and share their findings.

Multilevel Strategies

1 Preproduction
Give children two objects to weigh. Ask them to hold up the one that weighs more.

Writing Ask children to write down the weight of the two objects.

2 3 Early Production and Speech Emergence
Give children two objects to weigh. Ask them to tell you the results.

Writing Ask children to write a more than/less than sentence about one of the objects they weighed.

4 5 Intermediate and Advanced Fluency
Give children two objects to weigh. Ask them to explain step by step what they are doing.

Writing Ask children to write as many sentences as they can about the objects they weighed.

Name _____

The Best Unit

What is the best unit to use to weigh these objects?
Circle the unit of measure.

1. (ounce)　　　　pound	**2.** ounce　　　　pound
3. ounce　　　　pound	**4.** ounce　　　　pound
5. ounce　　　　pound	**6.** ounce　　　　pound

What is the best unit for measuring the mass of each
object? Draw a circle around it.

7. gram　　　　kilogram	**8.** gram　　　　kilogram
9. gram　　　　kilogram	**10.** gram　　　　kilogram

Lesson 4

45 minutes

▶ **Key Strategy**
Use visuals

▶ **Format**
Whole class

▶ **Math Vocabulary**
degrees Celsius (°C),
degrees Fahrenheit (°F),
temperature

▶ **Daily Vocabulary**
cold, comfortable, cool, hot,
scale, thermometer, warm

▶ **Resource**
Learning Resource 28
Teacher Tool 20

Materials
- glue
- markers
- old magazines for
  weather pictures
- scissors
- two large thermometers
  (Fahrenheit and Celsius)

Assessment

Check children's mastery of the
lesson vocabulary by observing
them as they read thermometers.
See Assessment Checklist on
page 115.

Home Connection

Ask children to work with a
family member to keep a record
of hot, warm, cool, or cold days
for one week, and share their
record with the class.

Measure Temperature

Math Objective	**ESL/TESOL Descriptors**
■ Read temperatures.	■ Practice new language. ■ Negotiate and manage interaction to accomplish tasks.

Activate Prior Knowledge Ask groups to find pictures of activities for a
temperature mural; e.g., diving (hot), skiing (cold), or biking (warm/cool). Have
children talk about the **temperature** in the pictures before gluing them.

Hands-on Lesson Display the Fahrenheit thermometer. Ask: *What do we
measure with a thermometer?* Tell them this thermometer measures temperature
in **degrees Fahrenheit** or **°F.** Explain how to read the marks for degrees. Point out
the sections: *hot, warm, cool,* and *cold,* and the freezing point, 32°.

- Hand out Teacher Tool 20: Fahrenheit Thermometer. Point to a picture on the
  mural. Ask: *What do you think the temperature is?* Ask children to look at the
  thermometer and make reasonable estimates. Then invite them to color the
  temperature on their thermometer, cut it out, and tape it under the picture.
  Continue until everyone has recorded a temperature.

- Display the Celsius thermometer. Discuss that temperature can also be measured
  in **degrees Celsius** or **°C.** Show that the freezing point is 0°.

- Hand out Teacher Tool 20: Celsius Thermometer and repeat the above activity.
  Hand out Learning Resource 28: Color the Temperature.

Challenge Assign *hot, warm, cool,* or *cold* to four children or groups. Invite them
to draw an activity they might do on that kind of day. Ask them to write a
reasonable temperature for that day in both Fahrenheit and Celsius.

Multilevel Strategies

1 Preproduction
Say the temperature from
one of the thermometers
on the mural and ask
children to find it.

Writing Say a temperature
and ask children to write if
it's hot, cold, warm, or cool.

**2 3 Early Production
and Speech Emergence**
Point to a thermometer on
the mural Ask: *What is
the temperature?*

Writing Point to a
thermometer on the
temperature mural and ask
children to write the
temperature.

**4 5 Intermediate
and Advanced Fluency**
Write 32°F on the board.
Ask: *What clothes
would you would wear
outside on a day with
this temperature?*

Writing Write a list of the
clothes you would wear.

Name _____

Color the Temperature

Read the temperature.

Color the thermometer to show the temperature.

1. 75°F

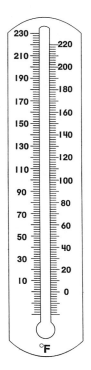

2. 45°F

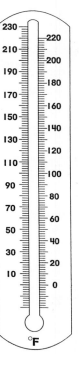

3. 35°C

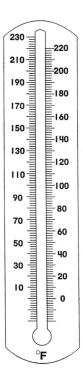

4. 55°C

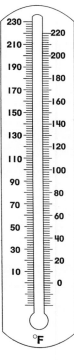

 45 minutes

▶ **Key Strategy**
Use manipulatives

▶ **Format**
Whole class and student pairs

▶ **Math Vocabulary**
angle, circle, cone, cube, cylinder, edge, face, hexagon, parallelogram, pentagon, rectangle, rectangular prism, pyramid, side, sphere, square, trapezoid, triangle, vertex, quadrilateral

▶ **Daily Vocabulary**
2-dimensional figures, 3-dimensional figures

▶ **Resource**
Learning Resource 29

Materials
- construction paper
- index cards
- markers
- multicolored squares
- pattern blocks
- sets of shapes

Assessment

Check children's mastery of the lesson vocabulary by observing them as they complete the lesson. See Assessment Checklist on page 115.

Home Connection

Encourage children to create a geometric drawing at home to share with the class.

2- and 3-Dimensional Figures

Math Objectives
- Identify 3-dimensional figures and their attributes.
- Identify 2-dimensional shapes and their attributes.

ESL/TESOL Descriptors
- Use context to construct meaning.
- Practice new language.

Activate Prior Knowledge Put 2-dimensional shapes and 3-dimensional figures on a table and ask children to sort them into two piles. Ask a child to pick a shape or figure and hold it up. Together, identify each item and its attributes. Create a word web for shapes and figures.

Hands-on Lesson Briefly review the attributes of 2-D shapes. Hold up each shape, count its sides and angles, say its name, and put it on a table. When you have finished with all the shapes, invite a volunteer to find the **triangle, pentagon, circle,** and so on.

- Ask a volunteer to stand facing the class. Put all the 2-D shapes on a table where the child can see them. Stand behind the child and write a shape name on the board. Ask the class to give clues about it. When the child guesses correctly, he or she sits down and another child takes a turn. Continue until all shapes have been identified correctly and children are comfortable identifying 2-D shapes.

- Briefly review the attributes of 3-D figures, pointing out an **edge, face,** and **vertex.** Then repeat the game activity described above until children are comfortable identifying 3-D figures. Ask children to review new vocabulary with their foldables.

- Hand out Learning Resource 29: Shape Patterns for pairs to complete.

Cultural Link Invite children to bring in illustrations of kites from different parts of the world. Ask what shapes children can see in the kites.

Multilevel Strategies

❶ Preproduction
Write *pentagon* on the board. Ask a volunteer to point to a pentagon on the table.

Writing Hold up a pentagon and ask children to write its name.

❷ ❸ Early Production and Speech Emergence
Hold up a pentagon and ask: ***What is this called? How many sides does it have?***

Writing Hold up a pentagon and ask children to write its name and how many sides it has.

❹ ❺ Intermediate and Advanced Fluency
Hold up a pentagon and ask children to describe it.

Writing Ask children to write a description of a pentagon.

Name _____

Shape Patterns!

Use △ ◯ ▢ ▢ to complete each pattern.

1.

◯ ◯ ◯ △ △ ◯ ◯ △ ___ ___ ___

2.

◯ ▢ △ ◯ ◯ ▢ △ ◯ ◯ ▢ ___ ___ ___ ___

3.

▢ △ ⬡ ◯ ▢ △ ⬡ ◯ ▢ ___ ___ ___ ___

4.

⏢ ▢ ▢ ⏢ ▢ ▢ ___ ___ ___ ___

Make your own pattern with a pentagon and two other shapes.

Lesson 6

 45 minutes

▶ **Key Strategy**
Use manipulatives

▶ **Format**
Whole class, small groups, and student pairs

▶ **Math Vocabulary**
area, congruent, flip, line of symmetry, perimeter, slide, turn

▶ **Daily Vocabulary**
equal parts, figure, half, units

▶ **Resources**
Teacher Tools 9 and 11

Materials
- construction paper
- inch ruler
- large index cards
- pattern blocks
- premade 2-D congruent paper shapes
- scissors

Assessment

Check children's mastery of the lesson vocabulary by observing them as they participate in the activities. See Assessment Checklist on page 115.

Home Connection

Encourage children show a family member how to draw a line of symmetry through a shape, such as a circle, square, rectangle, or triangle.

Spatial Concepts

Math Objectives	**ESL/TESOL Descriptors**
■ Identify congruent and symmetrical shapes.	■ Use context to construct meaning.
■ Identify slides, flips, and turns.	■ Understand and produce technical vocabulary.
■ Find the perimeter and area.	

Activate Prior Knowledge Hold up two triangles of different sizes. Put one on top of the other and ask children if they are the same. Repeat with two triangles the same size. Ask children what they can know about them. *(They are the same size and shape.)* Say: ***They are congruent.*** Hand out a variety of paper shapes to pairs, along with four index cards. Invite children to find two pairs of shapes that are the same size and shape and glue them onto the index cards.

Hands-on Lesson Model how to make a symmetrical figure. Hold up a piece of construction paper. Say: ***I can fold this paper in half.*** Fold paper in half, and draw half of a triangle using the fold as the line of symmetry. Then model how to cut along the drawn line and unfold. Say: ***This triangle has two equal parts.***

● Hand out paper and scissors to groups. Brainstorm with children some shapes they could draw, such as a rectangle, square, circle, pentagon, trapezoid, or hexagon. Draw each figure on the board and label.

● Have children in each group choose different figures. Work with them to fold their papers in half and draw half of the figure they chose. Ask children to cut out their shapes and unfold. Have them draw a line on the fold. Point out that this is a **line of symmetry** and that the two parts are **congruent** because they are the same size and shape.

● Combine groups and invite children to find a classmate who chose the same figure. Say: ***Compare your figures. Are they the same size and shape?*** Encourage children to put one figure on top of the other to see if they are the same size and shape. Ask: ***Are the figures congruent?*** Invite children to pin congruent figures on the bulletin board. Continue to combine different groups until everyone has compared their figures with different classmates.

● Hand out pattern blocks to pairs, along with Teacher Tool 11: Centimeter Graph Paper. Discuss with children that they can move figures in different ways. Write **slide, flip,** and **turn** on the board. Model how to slide, flip, and turn a triangle. You may want to draw this on the board so children can visualize how to move the figures.

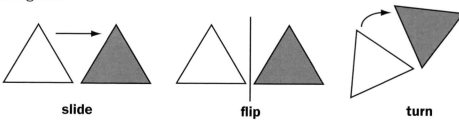

slide   flip   turn

● Invite children to trace a trapezoid on centimeter grid paper. Then ask them to move the trapezoid to show a slide, flip, and turn. Then encourage them to trace the trapezoid to show a slide, flip, and turn.

- Hold up a piece of 1-inch graph paper with one unit that is shaded, along with a shaded figure that is 5 units by 2 units. Point to one unit and say: ***This is one unit. I can find the distance around a shape, or its perimeter, by counting the units around the figure.*** Point to each unit as you count around figure in unison.

- Hand out Teacher Tool 9: Inch Graph Paper. Ask children to draw a rectangle that is 4 units long and 2 units wide. Ask: ***How can we find the perimeter?*** Say: ***Count the number of units around the shape. Start with the top left unit.*** Ask: ***How many units around is this shape?*** *(12)*

- Explain that there is another way to find the perimeter. Model how to do this. Say: ***I count the units on each side and then add.*** *(4 + 2 + 4 + 2 = 12)* Invite children to draw another rectangle or square and find the perimeter using their inch rulers.

- Hold up a sheet of centimeter graph paper with one square unit colored. Point to it and say: ***This is one square unit.*** It has an **area** of one square unit because it covers one square unit exactly. Invite children to draw a figure with area of 6 square units. Then invite them to draw figures that have areas of 5 square units, 7 square units, and 8 square units.

- Hand out centimeter graph paper and encourage children to draw as many figures as they can with a perimeter of 10 units. Then invite volunteers to share their work with the class.

Challenge Hand out centimeter graph paper and invite pairs to draw a symmetrical shape together. Then challenge children to draw a slide, flip, or turn of the shape that they drew.

Multilevel Strategies

1 Preproduction

Ask children to flip, slide, and turn a pattern block.

Writing Flip, slide, and turn a pattern block and ask children to write the word that describes your action.

2 3 Early Production and Speech Emergence

Flip, slide, and turn a pattern block and ask children to say what you are doing.

Writing Flip, slide, and turn a pattern block and ask children to write a sentence that describes your action.

4 5 Intermediate and Advanced Fluency

Ask children to explain how to move a shape to show a flip, slide, and turn.

Writing Ask children to write a description of how to move a shape to show a flip, slide, and turn.

Problem Solving

Problem Solving
Reading for Math

SKILL: Use Illustrations
Draw a pattern of 3 squares, 2 triangles, 4 circles, repeating twice on the board. Model the skill using a word problem such as the following:

1 Gia and Mark made a pattern with shapes. How many of each shape did they use? How many shapes did they use in all?

2 I can count how many of each shape they used. I can add to find how many shapes they used.

3 **Think:** How many squares do I see?
I see 6 squares.
Think: How many triangles do I see?
I see 4 triangles.
Think: How many circles do I see?
I see 8 circles.
I can follow my plan.
$6 + 4 + 8 = 18$ shapes.

4 I can check my answer by counting all the blocks.
There are 18 blocks.
Does my answer make sense? Yes.

Distribute **Math Center Card 5A** to children.

Math Center Card 5A

Reading for Math Skill

USE ILLUSTRATIONS • HOW FAR IS IT?

You need: drawing paper, crayons, ruler

1. You can draw a map about a story.
   Pick one of these stories:
   • Little Red Riding Hood on her way to Grandma's House.
   • Goldilocks on her way to the Three Bears's House.
   • The Wolf on his way to see the Three Little Pigs.

2. First draw a path for the story. Use a ruler to help you draw a line.

3. Next draw 3 things along the path. Space them apart.

4. Trade maps with your partner. Use a ruler to measure each part of the path.

5. How long is the whole path?

6. Check your partner's answers.

Math Center Card, Grade 2, Unit 5, 5A

STRATEGY: Guess and Check
Model the strategy using a word problem such as the following:

Read Jake put 12 seashells in boxes. Each box held 2 seashells. How many boxes did he use?

Plan I know each box holds 2 seashells. I know he has 12 shells. I can guess and check to find how many boxes.

Solve **First try:** 4 boxes. $2 + 2 + 2 + 2 = 8$. No.
Second try: 5 boxes. $2 + 2 + 2 + 2 + 2 = 10$. No.
Third try: 6 boxes. $2 + 2 + 2 + 2 + 2 + 2 = 12$. Yes.
Jake used 6 boxes.

Look Back Does my answer make sense?
Yes. How do I know?
$2 + 2 + 2 + 2 + 2 + 2 = 12$

Distribute **Math Center Card 5B** to children.

Math Center Card 5B

Problem Solving: Strategy

GUESS AND CHECK • HOW LONG IS THE YARN?

You need: yarn pieces, inch ruler

1. Put the yarn pieces in order—short, medium, long.
   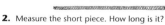
   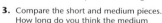
   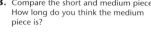

2. Measure the short piece. How long is it?

3. Compare the short and medium pieces. How long do you think the medium piece is?

4. Measure the medium piece. How long is it?

5. Put the short and medium pieces together. Compare them to the long piece. How long do you think the long piece is?
   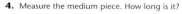

6. Measure the long piece. How long is it?

7. Did you guess right? What helped you guess?

Math Center Card, Grade 2, Unit 5, 5B

Assessment Checklist

	STUDENT NAMES								
SCHOOL:									
TEACHER: **SCHOOL YEAR:**									
Mark: + = **Mastery** √ = **Satisfactory** – = **Needs Improvement**									
LEVEL OF LANGUAGE PROFICIENCY (1–5)									
MATH OBJECTIVES									
• Identify congruent and symmetrical shapes.									
• Identify slides, flips, and turns.									
• Find the perimeter and area of a shape.									
• Measure length, width, and capacity in customary and metric units.									
• Read temperatures.									
• Identify 2- and 3-dimensional shapes and their attributes.									
ESL/TESOL LISTENING/SPEAKING									
Connect new information to information previously learned.									
Demonstrate knowledge through application.									
Observe and model how others speak in a particular situation.									
Select, connect, and explain information.									
Understand and produce technical vocabulary.									
ESL/TESOL READING									
Read about subject matter information.									
Apply basic reading comprehension skills.									
Follow written directions, implicit and explicit.									
ESL WRITING									
Write to demonstrate comprehension.									
Write using spelling patterns and targeted English vocabulary.									

Foldables

1 **Preproduction**
• Did children write the unit vocabulary?
• Did they copy the definitions?

2 **3** **Early Production and Speech Emergence**
• Did children label the tabs correctly?
• Did they write the vocabulary words?
• Did they copy the definitions?

4 **5** **Intermediate and Advanced Fluency**
• Did children write definitions for the unit vocabulary?
• Did they use correct spelling and grammar?

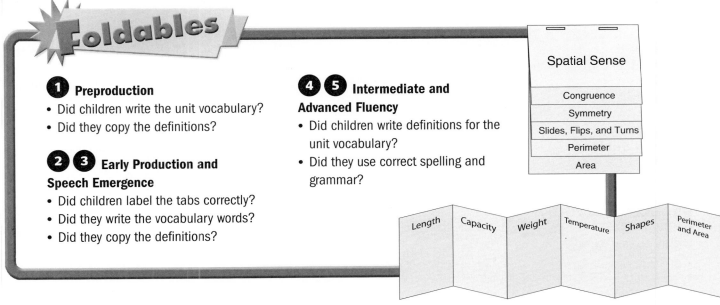

UNIT 6

Planner

Understanding Greater Numbers

Assessment
p. 137
• Assessment Checklist
• Foldables

LOG ON Visit **www.mmhmath.com**

Unit Activities

• **Activity 1** Readiness Number Riddles, p. 120
• **Activity 2** Greater or Less Than, p. 120
• **Activity 3** Subtraction Race, p. 121
• **Activity 4** To Regroup or Not to Regroup, p. 121

Lessons	Key Objectives	Vocabulary	Materials	Resources
READ TOGETHER "Math Is Brewing and I'm in Trouble" by Kalli Dakos, pp. 118–119	**Math:** Identify number patterns. **ESL/TESOL:** Goal 1/2, Standards 3/2.	brew, brewing, double, magic, millions, mix, stir, swirled, thousands, trouble		Graphic Organizer 1
UNIT WARM-UP Understanding Numbers to 1,000 p. 122	**Math:** Count, read, write, and represent numbers to 1,000. **ESL/TESOL:** Goal 1/2, Standards 3/1.	tens, hundreds, thousand	base-ten, hundreds, connecting cubes	**Overhead Manipulatives**
LESSON 1 Place Value to Thousands pp. 124–125	**Math:** Identify place value for each digit for numbers to 1,000. **ESL/TESOL:** Goal 1, Standard 3.	digit, expanded form, place value, thousands	paper clips, small plastic bags	Learning Resource 30 Teacher Tool 8
LESSON 2 Numbers to 1,000 pp. 126–127	**Math:** Compare and order numbers to 1,000. Identify number patterns. **ESL/TESOL:** Goal 1, Standard 3.	is equal to (=), is greater than (>), is less than (<)	index cards with 3-digit numbers, index cards with <, >, = symbols	Learning Resource 31 Teacher Tool 1
LESSON 3 Sets of Numbers to 1,000 pp. 128–129	**Math:** Compare and order numbers to 1,000. Identify number patterns. **ESL/TESOL:** Goal 2, Standard 1.	count back, count on, greater than, greatest, least, less than	index cards with numbers between 100–1,000	Learning Resource 32
LESSON 4 Add Hundreds, Tens, and Ones pp. 130–131	**Math:** Regroup ones or tens to add 3-digit numbers. **ESL/TESOL:** Goal 1, Standard 3.	addend, regroup	index cards, place-value charts	Learning Resource 33 Teacher Tool 8
LESSON 5 Subtract 3-Digit Numbers pp. 132–133	**Math:** Regroup tens or hundreds to subtract 3-digit numbers. **ESL/TESOL:** Goal 1, Standard 3.	difference, regroup	base-ten set, index cards, place-value charts	Learning Resource 34 Teacher Tool 8
LESSON 6 Add and Subtract Money pp. 134–135	**Math:** Add and subtract money amounts. **ESL/TESOL:** Goal 2/1, Standards 3/3.	decimal point, dollar sign, estimate, place, round down, round up	classroom objects with price tags between $1.00 and $9.99	Learning Resource 35
PROBLEM SOLVING p. 136 • Skill: Make Predictions • Strategy: Make a Table	Use skills and strategies to solve problems.			**Math Center Cards 6A, 6B**

See **Math at Home Familly Guide** for additional math vocabulary, activities, and games in English, Spanish, and Haitian Creole.

English Vocabulary

Dear Family: Please help your child practice the key vocabulary words for this unit.

digit one of the numerals 0, 1, 2, 3, 4, 5, 6, 7, 8, or 9

expanded form a number written as an addition, showing the value of each digit

hundreds the third digit from the right in a whole number

is greater than has a larger value than; shown by the symbol >

is less than has a smaller value than; shown by the symbol <

ones the numbers 0 through 9; the first right-hand digit in whole numbers greater than 9

tens the second digit from the right in a whole number greater than 9

Vocabulario en español

Estimados familiares: Por favor ayuden a su hijo/a a practicar las palabras del vocabulario de esta unidad.

dígito uno de los números 0, 1, 2, 3, 4, 5, 6, 7, 8, 9

forma desarrollada número escrito como suma, que muestra el valor de cada dígito

centenas el tercer dígito desde la derecha de un número entero

mayor que vale más que; se representa con el símbolo >

menor que vale menos que; se representa con el símbolo <

unidades los números del 0 al 9; el primer dígito de la derecha de un número entero mayor que 9

decenas el segundo dígito de la derecha en un número entero mayor que 9

Vokabilè an kreyol

Chè paran: Tanpri ede pitit la pratike mo vokabilè nan seksyon sa a.

chif youn pami chif 0, 1, 2, 3, 4, 5, 6, 7, 8, 9

fòm dekonpoze se yon nonb ki ekri sou fòm yon adisyon, ki montre valè chak chif

santèn se twazyèm chif ki agòch yon nonb antye

pi gran pase ki gen yon pi gwo valè pase; reprezante pa senbòl >

pi piti pase piti valè pase; reprezante pa senbòl <

inite se nonb 0 jiska 9; se premye chif ki adwat nonb antye ki pi gran pase 9

dizèn se dezyèm chif ki agòch yon nonb antye ki pi gran pase 9

© Macmillan/McGraw-Hill

Math at Home

MATH IS BREWING AND I'M IN TROUBLE

by Kalli Dakos

 30 minutes

Math Objective
- Identify number patterns.

ESL/TESOL Descriptors
- Listen to and imitate how others use English.
- Listen to, speak, read, and write about subject matter.

Reading Skill
- Draw conclusions.

Vocabulary
brew, brewing, double, magic, millions, mix, stir, swirled, thousands, trouble

Before Reading

Build Background/Oral Language
Read the title of the poem. Hand out index cards. Invite each child to write a number. Collect the cards and put them in a big pot. Use a big wooden spoon and stir the numbers to demonstrate brewing.

During Reading

- Read the poem through once without stopping. Encourage children to ask about new or difficult words.
- Read the poem again, pausing after each line for children to repeat after you. Encourage children to draw a conclusion from what they have read by asking: **What does the writer want to do? Why?**
- Read the poem in unison.

Phonological/Phonemic Awareness
Draw attention to the /ə/ sound at the end of *single* and *double*. Ask children to find another word that ends in the same sound. *(trouble)*

After Reading

Hand out the Graphic Organizer 1: Word Web. Invite children to read the poem to find the words that name numbers. Ask them to copy the words onto their word webs and add some more words of their own.

Art Invite children to draw pictures that show themselves brewing a pot of something that they would like to make disappear. Invite children to discuss their pictures.

Assessment

Observe children's participation as you read the poem. See Assessment Checklist on page 137.

Multilevel Strategies

1 Preproduction
Say: **Draw circles around the number words in the poem.**

Writing Ask children to make number cards to match the words they circled.

2 3 Early Production and Speech Emergence
Say: **What are the number words in the poem?**

Writing Invite children to make a list of the number words in the poem.

4 5 Intermediate and Advanced Fluency
Ask: **What numbers are the "numbers single" in the poem?**

Writing Invite children to write a list of "numbers double" that could be put into the brew.

MATH IS BREWING AND I'M IN TROUBLE

by Kalli Dakos

Someone is brewing
something very strange in this poem.

Numbers single,

Numbers double,

Math is brewing

And I'm in trouble.

If I could mix a magic brew,

Numbers, I'd take care of you!

First, I'd mix in one, two, three,

And one, two, three no more would be.

Then I'd take four, five, and six,

And mix until the brew was thick.

I'd stir and add and stir some more—

One hundred, two hundred, three hundred, four.

As thousands and millions boiled and swirled,

I'd think of how I'd saved the world.

67

6

240

8,963

Activities

Activities

Readiness

ACTIVITY 1

PARTNERS

Number Riddles

Take turns.

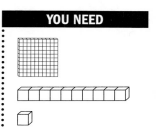

YOU NEED

- Write a 3-digit number on a piece of paper. Do not show your partner the paper.

- Use models to show the number. Use hundreds, tens, and ones.

- Show your partner your models. Ask your partner to write the number on a piece of paper.

- If your partner's answer is right, then he or she makes a number with models for you to guess.

Represent Numbers to 1,000

ACTIVITY 2

INDIVIDUAL

Greater or Less Than

YOU NEED

number cards

9

9

9

paper bag

- Put all the number cards in the bag. Take out 3 cards. Make a 3-digit number.

- Take out 3 more cards. Make another 3-digit number.

- Show the numbers with hundreds, tens, and ones. Write the numbers. Compare. Write > or <.

- Put the cards back in the bag and do this again 4 more times.

Bonus: Can you write all of your numbers in order from least to greatest?

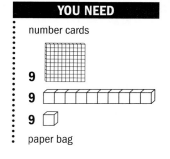

347

Compare Numbers to 1,000

ACTIVITY 3

Grab Bag

Take turns.

- Take some coins from the bag.
  Sort the dimes, nickels, and pennies.

- Write how much money you have.
  Your partner checks your total.
  Put the coins back in the bag.

Each of you plays 4 times.
Check your partner's work.

YOU NEED

20

8

5

a bag

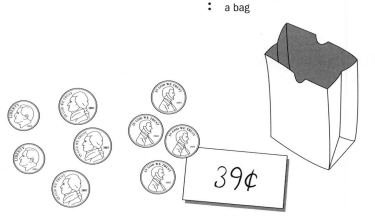

Add Money Amounts

ACTIVITY 4

INDIVIDUAL

To Regroup or Not to Regroup

- Roll the cube three times for three numbers. Write them to make a 3-digit number. Show this number with the models.

- Write a number to take away. Use the model to show how you take it away. Did you have to regroup?

- Start again with the same 3-digit number.

- Take away a number so that you must regroup.

- Try again. This time, do not regroup.

YOU NEED

6

12

12

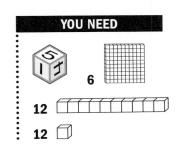

265 − 142 = 123

Regroup to Subtract 3-Digit Numbers

© Macmillan/McGraw-Hill

 30 minutes

▶ Key Strategy
Use manipulatives

▶ Format
Whole class and small groups

▶ Math Vocabulary
hundreds, tens, thousand

▶ Daily Vocabulary
count by, group, skip-count

▶ Resource
Overhead Manipulatives: Base-Ten Set

▶ Materials
base-ten hundreds, connecting cubes

Understanding Numbers to 1,000

Activate Prior Knowledge Display a pile of 100 connecting cubes. Ask: ***How can we group these cubes to count them quickly?*** *(put the cubes in groups of tens)* Invite volunteers to make groups of **ten**. Ask: ***How many groups of ten are there?*** *(10)* Ask: ***What is a fast way to count these groups?*** *(skip-count by 10s)* Skip-count by tens together. Ask: ***How many cubes are there in all?*** *(100)* You may want to use Overhead Manipulatives: Base-Ten set to reinforce children's understanding.

Hands-on Lesson Give each child a base-ten hundred model. Put children in groups of varied sizes. Ask: ***How many hundreds does your group have?*** Ask a group to stand up in a row and to count on by hundreds. *(one hundred, two hundred …)* Repeat with other groups.

● Combine groups, ensuring that at least one group has ten children. Repeat the activity, counting greater numbers of hundreds. When each group finishes counting, ask a volunteer to write the total on the board. Point out that 10 hundreds = 1 **thousand** and that we write it as 1,000. Continue until children are comfortable counting on by hundreds.

● Display three base-ten hundred blocks. Ask: ***How many hundreds?*** *(3)* ***How many tens?*** *(30)* ***How many ones?*** *(300)* Display a variety of hundreds blocks. Ask volunteers to write how many hundreds, tens, and ones.

● If children have difficulty, model how they can find the answer. Hold up two base-ten hundred blocks. Say: ***I can find how many hundreds by counting by hundreds. I can find how many tens by counting by tens.***

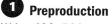

Multilevel Strategies

❶ Preproduction
Write *400, 500,* and *600* on the board. Point to *500.* Ask children to hold up the correct number of hundreds.

❷❸ Early Production and Speech Emergence
Write *400, 500,* and *600* on the board. Point to *500.* Ask children to name it and hold up the correct number of hundreds.

❹❺ Intermediate and Advanced Fluency
Hold up random numbers of hundreds models and ask children to name them.

 Visit **www.mmhmath.com** to find printable **Vocabulary Cards** that help build academic language.

Procedure: Help children make these Foldables to write vocabulary words and definitions throughout the unit. Encourage children to use the Foldables as a study guide.

Folded Table

1. Provide each child with a sheet of 11" × 17" or 12" × 18" paper, or use a 4-foot-long sheet of bulletin-board paper to make one giant table to be used by the class.

2. Fold the selected paper into fourths to form four rows.

3. Open and fold into fourths again, forming 4 columns and 16 rectangles. Label as illustrated.

4. Trace along the fold lines.

5. As children progress through the unit, have them take notes and record information in the appropriate columns of their table.

Labels may include:

	Add Hundreds	Regroup Ones	Regroup Tens
Examples			
Describe			
Describe			

Going Further Children can use their Folded Tables to review by comparing their pictures and examples of 3-digit addition.

Three-Tab Book

1. Provide each child with a sheet of 11" × 17" paper or use a sheet of poster board to make one large classroom Three-Tab Book.

2. Fold the paper or poster board like a hot dog, but make one side longer, as illustrated.

3. Make two cuts equal distances apart on the short side of the paper. Label the tabs.

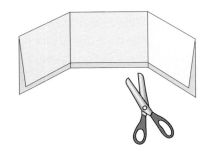

4. As you work through the unit, have students record information they learn under the appropriate tabs of the Three-Tab Book.

5. Don't forget to include math words, definitions, symbols, and examples of numbers to 1,000 under the tabs.

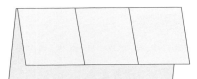

Place value to the thousands	Compare and Order Numbers to 1,000	Order Sets of Numbers to 1,000

Numbers to 1,000

Going Further Children can use the Three-Tab Book to review by comparing their pictures and examples of probability. They can also create another Three-Tab Book to make an organized list of a home- or school-related subject.

⏱ **45 minutes**

▶ **Key Strategy**
Use manipulatives

▶ **Format**
Whole class and student pairs

▶ **Math Vocabulary**
digit, expanded form, place value, thousands

▶ **Daily Vocabulary**
column, groups

▶ **Resources**
Learning Resource 30
Teacher Tool 8

Materials
- paper clips (more then 100 for each pair)
- small plastic bags

Assessment

Check children's mastery of the lesson vocabulary by observing them as they complete the lesson. See page 137 for Assessment Checklist. Remind children to work on their Foldables.

Home Connection

Have children take home their Learning Resource page to share. Ask them to work with a family member to draw another hundreds problem to share with the class.

Place Value to Thousands

Math Objectives	ESL/TESOL Descriptors
■ Count, read, write, and represent numbers to 1,000. ■ Identify place value for each digit for numbers to 1,000.	■ Use context to construct meaning. ■ Practice new language.

Activate Prior Knowledge Give pairs paper clips and bags. Ask: *How can we group the paper clips to count 100 easily?* (group by 10s) Ask children to put 10 groups of ten in bags to make 100. Display 10 bags of 100 clips each. Ask: *How many bags of 100 clips do we need to make 1,000?* (10) *How many bags of 10 clips?* (100) *How many bags of one paper clip?* (1,000)

Hands-on Lesson Distribute Teacher Tool 8 to pairs. Write *346*. Point to each digit. Say: *I can tell the place value of a digit by its place in the number. I have 3 hundreds, 4 tens, and 6 ones.* Say: *If I know the number of hundreds, the number of tens, and the number of ones, I know the number—346.* Have children place 3, 4, and 6 in the correct column on their place-value mats.

● Say: *I can write 346 another way.* Write and say: *300 + 40 + 1 is the same as 346, but it is in expanded form.* Write other numbers. Have children write each number in expanded form.

● Write *1,368* in a labeled place-value chart on the board. Point to and say each place-value name on the chart. Ask: *What digit is in the thousands place? In the hundreds place? In the tens place? In the ones place?* Write other 4-digit numbers on the board. Ask children to identify the place value of each digit.

● Give children Learning Resource 30 to complete.

Challenge Have pairs write 4-digit riddles and exchange with other pairs. For example: *"My number has 2 in the thousands place, 5 in the hundreds place, 6 in the tens place, and 4 in the ones place. What is it?"* (2,564)

Multilevel Strategies

① Preproduction
Write *578*. Say: *Draw a circle around the digit that shows how many hundreds are in the number 578.*

Writing Say 3- and 4-digit numbers. Ask children to write them.

② ③ Early Production and Speech Emergence
Write *578*. Ask: *What is the digit that shows how many hundreds are in the number 578?*

Writing Say 3- and 4-digit numbers. Ask children to write them in expanded form.

④ ⑤ Intermediate and Advanced Fluency
Ask children to describe a number to a partner: *It has 2 thousands, 6 hundreds, 5 tens, and 9 ones.*

Writing Ask children to write the number their partner described to them.

Name _____

How Many Hundreds?

Count the hundreds. Then write the number.

1.

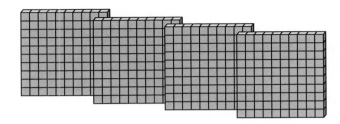

_____

2.

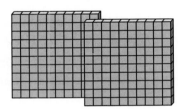

_____

3.

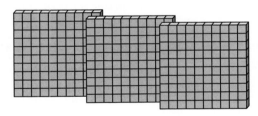

_____

4.

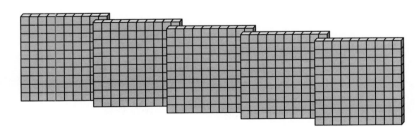

_____

5.

_____

 45 minutes

▶ **Key Strategy**
Use visuals

▶ **Format**
Whole class and student pairs

▶ **Math Vocabulary**
is equal to (=), is greater than (>), is less than (<)

▶ **Daily Vocabulary**
compare, order

▶ **Resources**
Learning Resource 31
Teacher Tool 1

Materials
• index cards with a variety of 3-digit numbers
• index cards with <, >, = symbols

Assessment

Check children's mastery of the lesson vocabulary by observing them as they compare numbers. See page 137 for Assessment Checklist. Remind children to work on their Foldables.

Home Connection

Have children take home their Learning Resource page to share. Ask them to work with a family member to make up three new problems to share with the class.

Numbers to 1,000

Math Objectives	**ESL/TESOL Descriptors**
■ Compare and order numbers to 1,000. ■ Identify number patterns.	■ Use context to construct meaning. ■ Negotiate and manage interaction to complete tasks.

Activate Prior Knowledge Display number cards 0–9. Ask a child to make a 3-digit number and write it on the board. Ask: *How many tens are in this number? How many ones?* Repeat with another volunteer and 3-digit number. Then ask: *Which number is the greatest? How do you know?*

Hands-on Lesson Write *346* and *355* on the board. Ask: *Which number is the largest, or greatest?* Say: *First look at the place value of the hundreds. If the hundreds are the same, look at the value of the tens. If the tens are the same, look at the value of the ones.* Elicit that 355 is larger, or **greater than** 346 and show how to write this as *355 > 346*. Follow up by saying 346 is smaller, or **less than** 355. Show how to write this as *346 < 355*.

• Give pairs index cards with 3-digit numbers and symbols $<$, $>$, $=$. Write each symbol on the board with its meaning: *is greater than, is less than,* and is **equal to.**

• Children in pairs each choose a card. Say: *Put the cards in order so the greater number is first. Then choose the symbol that shows the first number is greater than the second.* ($>$) Ask one child to put the $>$ card between the numbers. Then say: *Now put the cards in order so that the smaller, or lesser, number is first.* Have the other child put the $<$ between the numbers.

• Have children continue with other cards. Then hand out Learning Resource 31 for children to complete.

Challenge Pairs place number cards face down. Each child chooses 3 cards and makes the largest number possible. The child with the largest number gets 1 point. Pairs return cards to pile and shuffle. The first player to get 10 points wins.

Multilevel Strategies

1 Preproduction
Write two 3-digit numbers. Say: *Point to the number that is greater.*

Writing Ask children to write the symbol that means greater than.

2 3 Early Production and Speech Emergence
Write two 3-digit numbers. Ask: *Which number is greater?*

Writing Ask children to write the two numbers in a sentence with >.

4 5 Intermediate and Advanced Fluency
Write two 3-digit numbers. Ask children to use them in sentences that include *greater than* and *less than*.

Writing Ask children to write their sentences.

Name _____

Compare Numbers

Compare the numbers. Write $<$, $>$, or $=$.

1. 345 _____ 334   2. 845 _____ 865   3. 433 _____ 433

4. 907 _____ 977   5. 143 _____ 123   6. 312 _____ 314

7. 677 _____ 677   8. 562 _____ 561   9. 367 _____ 368

10. 555 _____ 545   11. 921 _____ 921   12. 400 _____ 300

Write the words **is greater than, is less than,** or **is equal to**.

13. 239 _____ 293

14. 202 _____ 202

15. 407 _____ 400

16. 999 _____ 899

Lesson 3

45 minutes

▶ **Key Strategy**
Use visuals

▶ **Format**
Whole class and student pairs

▶ **Math Vocabulary**
count on, count back, greater than, greatest, least, less than

▶ **Daily Vocabulary**
between, just after, just before, order, set

▶ **Resource**
Learning Resource 32

Materials
• index cards with numbers between 100–1,000

Sets of Numbers to 1,000

Math Objectives	**ESL/TESOL Descriptors**
■ Compare and order numbers to 1,000. ■ Identify number patterns.	■ Participate in full class, group, and pair discussions. ■ Negotiate and manage interaction to accomplish tasks.

Activate Prior Knowledge Draw a number line from 30–50. Circle 46. Ask: *What number comes just before 46? Just after?* Help children recall using a number line can help them order numbers. Write *39* and *41*. Ask: *What number comes between 39 and 41?* Invite children to make up similar questions to answer.

Hands-on Lesson Draw a number line from 245–255. Omit 247, 251, and 254. Ask: *How can you find out the number just before 248?* (count back one) *How can you find the number just after 252?* (count on one) *How can you find the number that comes between 253 and 255?* (count on or back one)

• Give pairs 6 number cards. Ask each child to put 3 cards in order from least to greatest and then from greatest to least. Mix up cards and repeat.

• Write *810*. Have children count by tens to 1,000 as you write the numbers. Write *100*. Have children count by hundreds to 1,000. Write *250*. Have children count by 50s to 1,000.

• Display a number line from 130–170. Ask: *What counting pattern does this number line show?* (tens) Say: *I can count on by tens and count back by tens.* Have the class count on and back in unison. Supervise children as they solve the activity on Learning Resource 32.

Challenge Have pairs put four 3-digit number cards in order from greatest to least. Combine into groups of four and put the numbers in order from greatest to least. Continue with larger groups until there is one set of numbers.

Multilevel Strategies

1 Preproduction
Using the number line from the Hands-on Lesson, say: *Point to the number that comes just before 249 on the number line.*

Writing Ask children to write the number that comes between 248 and 250.

2 3 Early Production and Speech Emergence
Ask: *What number comes just before 249?*

Writing Ask children to complete: _____ comes just before 247.

4 5 Intermediate and Advanced Fluency
Ask children to ask a partner questions like *What number comes just before 249?*

Writing Ask children to write sentences that say what numbers come just before and just after 247.

Name _____

Number Challenge

Write the numbers in order from least to greatest. Use the number line to help.

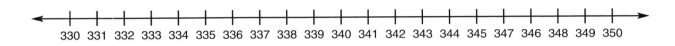

330 331 332 333 334 335 336 337 338 339 340 341 342 343 344 345 347 346 348 349 350

1. 335, 331, 339   _____, _____, _____

2. 350, 338, 345   _____, _____, _____

3. 340, 330, 350   _____, _____, _____

4. 349, 336, 332   _____, _____, _____

5. 343, 341, 342   _____, _____, _____

6. 339, 348, 345   _____, _____, _____

Now try writing these numbers in order from least to greatest.

7. 450, 550, 350, 250   _____, _____, _____, _____

8. 730, 710, 720, 740   _____, _____, _____, _____

9. 600, 800, 900, 700   _____, _____, _____, _____

10. 901, 904, 902, 903   _____, _____, _____, _____

▶ **Key Strategy**
Use manipulatives

▶ **Format**
Whole class and student pairs

▶ **Math Vocabulary**
addend, regroup

▶ **Daily Vocabulary**
column

▶ **Resources**
Learning Resource 33
Teacher Tool 8

Materials
- base-ten sets
- index cards with 3-digit addition problems regrouping ones and tens
- place-value chart

Assessment

Check children's mastery of the lesson by observing them while they participate in the activities. See page 137 for Assessment Checklist. Remind children to work on their Foldables.

Home Connection

Have children take home their Learning Resource pages to share. Ask them to work with a family member to create a new addition problem to share with the class.

Add Hundreds, Tens, and Ones

Math Objective	**ESL/TESOL Descriptors**
■ Regroup ones or tens to add three-digit numbers.	■ Practice new language. ■ Use context to construct meaning.

Activate Prior Knowledge Skip-count by hundreds from 100–900. Write the numbers to make a number line. Point out knowing basic facts can help us add hundreds. Write *400 + 200*. Say: ***400 + 200 is the same as 4 hundreds and 2 hundreds. 4 + 2 is 6, so 400 + 200 = 600.***

Hands-on Lesson Give pairs base-ten sets and Teacher Tool 8: Place-Value Workmats. Write *223 + 148* in a place-value chart. Have pairs show 223 and 148 in the correct columns on their mats.

● Model 223 + 148. Say: ***First, I add the ones. If there are more than ten ones, I regroup 10 ones as a ten.*** Model regrouping 10 ones. Have children make a 10 and move it to the tens column. Add the ones. Say: ***Next, I add the tens.*** Ask: ***How many tens are there?*** (7) ***Do I need to regroup?*** (no) Add the tens. Then say: ***Last, I can add the hundreds.*** Add the hundreds. Repeat, modeling 142 + 671.

● Hand out the index cards. Have pairs write the problem, model it, and add. Hand out Learning Resource 33. *(Answers: 1. 582; 2. 792; 3. 580; 4. 696; 5. 713; 6. 435; 7. 586; 8. 948)*

Challenge Ask pairs to choose three 3-digit numbers between 100–220 and three 3-digit numbers between 226–450, and use them to write and solve as many problems as they can.

Multilevel Strategies

① Preproduction
Point to 125 + 322 and 151 + 352 and ask children to nod if they need to regroup.

Writing Ask children to find the sums and write *regroup* or *do not regroup*.

② ③ Early Production and Speech Emergence
Point to 125 + 322 and 151 + 352 and ask children if they need to regroup.

Writing Ask children to find the sums and write a sentence that says if they regrouped.

④ ⑤ Intermediate and Advanced Fluency
Ask children to explain how they decide if they need to regroup in 125 + 322 and 151 + 352.

Writing Ask children to write the steps for regrouping.

33

Name _____

Add Hundreds, Tens, and Ones

Add.

1.

hundreds	tens	ones
4	5	6
+ 1	2	6

5.

hundreds	tens	ones
3	5	2
+ 3	6	1

2.

hundreds	tens	ones
1	2	3
+ 5	6	9

6.

hundreds	tens	ones
1	8	4
+ 5	3	3

3.

hundreds	tens	ones
4	5	4
+ 1	2	6

7.

hundreds	tens	ones
2	9	4
+ 2	9	2

4.

hundreds	tens	ones
3	7	8
+ 3	1	8

8.

hundreds	tens	ones
4	5	1
+ 4	9	7

© Macmillan/McGraw-Hill

Lesson 5

 45 minutes

▶ **Key Strategy**
Use manipulatives

▶ **Format**
Whole class and student pairs

▶ **Math Vocabulary**
difference, regroup

▶ **Daily Vocabulary**
column, first, last, next

▶ **Resources**
Learning Resource 34
Teacher Tool 8

Materials
- hundreds, tens, ones models (base-ten set)
- index cards with 3-digit subtraction problems regrouping tens and ones
- place-value chart
- tic-tac-toe grids

Assessment

Check children's mastery of the lesson by observing them as they complete the lesson. See page 137 for Assessment Checklist. Remind children to work on their Foldables.

Home Connection

Have children take home their Learning Resource pages to share. Ask them to work with a family member to make up a subtraction problem to share with the class.

132 Unit 6 • Lesson 5

Subtract 3-Digit Numbers

Math Objective	**ESL/TESOL Descriptors**
■ Regroup tens or hundreds to subtract 3-digit numbers.	■ Practice new language. ■ Use context to construct meaning.

Activate Prior Knowledge Skip-count by hundreds backward from 1,000–100. Write the numbers to make a number line. Point out knowing basic facts can help us subtract hundreds. Write *600 − 300.* **6 hundreds − 3 hundreds. 6 − 3 is 3, so 600 − 300 = 300.**

Hands-on Lesson Give pairs base-ten sets and Teacher Tool 8: Place-Value Workmats. Write *345 − 126* in a place-value chart. Have pairs show 345 and 126 on their mats.

● Model 345 − 126. Say: ***First, I subtract the ones. If there are not enough ones, I regroup.*** Model regrouping 1 ten as 10 ones. Have children move a 10 to the ones column. Subtract the ones. Say: ***Next, I subtract the tens. Last, I subtract the hundreds.*** Repeat, modeling 643 − 251.

● Hand out the index cards. Have pairs write the problem, model it, and subtract. Hand out Learning Resource 34. *(Answers: 1. 419; 2. 216; 3. 328; 4. 438; 5. 353; 6. 156; 7. 573; 8. 491)*

Challenge Ask pairs to choose three 3-digit numbers between 100–500 and three 3-digit numbers between 501–999, and use them to write and solve as many problems as they can.

Multilevel Strategies

❶ Preproduction
Point to *223 − 148* and *348 − 136* and ask children to nod if they need to regroup.

Writing Invite children to find the differences and write *regroup* or *do not regroup.*

❷ ❸ Early Production and Speech Emergence
Point to *223 − 148* and *348 − 136* and ask: **Do you need to regroup?**

Writing Ask children to find the differences and write a sentence that says if they regrouped.

❹ ❺ Intermediate and Advanced Fluency
Ask children to explain how they decide if they need to regroup in *223 − 148* and *348 − 136.*

Writing Ask children to write the steps for regrouping.

Name _____

Subtract Hundreds, Tens, and Ones

Subtract the numbers.

1.

hundreds	tens	ones
5	4	6
− 1	2	7

5.

hundreds	tens	ones
5	1	4
− 1	6	1

2.

hundreds	tens	ones
3	4	4
− 1	2	8

6.

hundreds	tens	ones
4	3	8
− 2	8	2

3.

hundreds	tens	ones
4	5	4
− 1	2	6

7.

hundreds	tens	ones
9	4	4
− 3	7	1

4.

hundreds	tens	ones
7	5	6
− 3	1	8

8.

hundreds	tens	ones
6	7	7
− 1	8	6

Lesson

6

 45 minutes

▶ **Key Strategy**
Use visuals

▶ **Format**
Whole class and student pairs

▶ **Math Vocabulary**
decimal point, dollar sign, estimate, place, round down, round up

▶ **Daily Vocabulary**
amount, nearest, price tag, reasonable

▶ **Resource**
Learning Resource 35

Materials
- small classroom objects with price tags between $1.00 and $9.99

Assessment

Check children's mastery of the lesson by observing them adding and subtracting money amounts. See page 137 for Assessment Checklist. Remind children to work on their Foldables.

Home Connection

Have children take home their Learning Resource pages to share. Ask them to work with a family member to create a new problem to share with the class.

Add and Subtract Money

Math Objective	**ESL/TESOL Descriptors**
■ Add and subtract money amounts.	■ Connect new information to information previously learned. ■ Practice new language.

Activate Prior Knowledge Draw a number line from 0–10. Put a ● on 5. Remind children when we round a number to the nearest 10, we look at the number in the ones place first. If the number is 4 or less, we **round down** to the nearest 10. If the number is 5 or more, we **round up** to the nearest 10.

Hands-on Lesson Draw a number line from 200–300 by tens. Put a ● on 250. Say: *When we round to the nearest hundred, we look at the number in the tens place. If it is 5 or more, we round up. If it is 4 or less, we round down.*

- Add a **dollar sign** and **decimal point** to each number on the number line. Explain rounding money amounts is the same as rounding whole numbers. Point to $2.20. Ask: *What number is in the tens place? Do we round up or down? Is $2.20 nearest $2.00 or nearest $3.00?* Repeat with other amounts. Explain knowing how to round can help us make **reasonable estimates.**

- Have pairs to choose two objects with price tags and estimate the total by rounding the prices to the nearest dollar. Remind them to line up decimal points. Ask the pairs to find the difference between the two prices. Hand out Learning Resource 35. *(Answers: 1. $4.46; 2. $1.50; 3. $6.00; 4. $2.55, $5.00)*

Challenge Ask pairs to make a list of items they could buy with $10.00.

Cultural Link Invite children to bring in foreign coins and currency the next day. Have a "Show and Tell" activity.

Multilevel Strategies

❶ Preproduction
Point to *$2.60* on the number line. Say: *Point to the nearest dollar.*

Writing Ask children to round $2.60 to the nearest dollar.

❷ ❸ Early Production and Speech Emergence
Point to *$2.60* on the number line. Ask: *What is the nearest dollar?*

Writing Ask children to round $2.60 to the nearest dollar and write *round up.*

❹ ❺ Intermediate and Advanced Fluency
Write *$2.60* and ask children how they decide if they need to round up or round down.

Writing Have children write directions for rounding up to the nearest dollar.

Name _____

Add and Subtract Money

Solve each problem below.

ROUND AND ESTIMATE	SOLVE
1. Eric went to the store with $5.21 and brought a candy bar for $0.75. How much money did he have left over? I estimate _____.	
2. At a baseball game, drinks cost $2.00 and peanuts cost $1.75 for a bag. If you buy one drink and 2 bags of peanuts, how much change should you have from $7.00? I estimate _____.	
3. Your neighbor pays you $3.00 to mow the lawn and $1.50 to collect the mail for a week. If you collect the mail for two weeks and mow the lawn once, how much money will you earn? I estimate _____.	
4. Nathan has $7.55 and Alex has $2.45. Admission to the movies is $5.00. How much should Nathan loan Alex? How much will Nathan have left? I estimate _____.	

Problem Solving
Reading for Math

SKILL: Make Predictions

Model the skill using a word problem such as the following:

1 There are 5 juice box cartons on the shelf. Matt opens one carton. There are 3 juice boxes in each carton. How many juice boxes are on the shelf?

2 I can predict how many juice boxes there are in all.
I know that one carton has 3 juice boxes.
I know that there are 5 cartons.
I can skip-count to solve.

3 I can carry out my plan.
I can skip-count by threes.
3, 6, 9, 12, 15
There will be 15 juice boxes on the shelf.

4 I'll check my answer by making a model with counters.
Does my answer make sense?

Distribute **Math Center Card 6A** to children.

Math Center Card 6A

Reading for Math Skill

MAKE PREDICTIONS • PREDICT HOW MANY

You need: boxes of crayons

With a partner, read the story and answer the questions.

There are 10 boxes of crayons on the table.
Tim opens a box.
He sees 8 crayons.
Tim predicts there are 80 crayons in all.

1. Why did Tim predict 80 crayons in all?
2. Why might his prediction be wrong?
3. How could Tim check his prediction?

Math Center Card, Grade 2, Unit 6, 6A

STRATEGY: Make a Table

Model the strategy using a word problem such as the following:

Read Ben has a new sticker book. It has 5 pages. He puts 6 stickers on each page. How many stickers will be in the book?

Plan I know that each page had 6 stickers.
I know that there are 5 pages.
I can use a table to solve.

Solve

pages	1	2	3	4	5
stickers	6	12	18	24	30

There will be 30 stickers in the book.

Look Back I'll check my answer by making a model with counters.
Does my answer make sense?
Yes.

Distribute **Math Center Card 6B** to children.

Math Center Card 6B

Problem Solving: Strategy

MAKE A TABLE • LUNCH TIME TABLE

1. Work with a partner. Read the story.
The students at school ate lots of sandwiches. They ate 35 peanut butter sandwiches, 15 cheese sandwiches, and 20 tuna sandwiches. How many sandwiches did they eat in all?

2. Copy and complete the table. Show how many peanut butter, cheese, and tuna sandwiches the students ate.

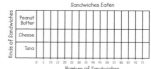

3. How many sandwiches did the students eat in all?
4. How does the table help you solve the problem?

Math Center Card, Grade 2, Unit 6, 6B

Assessment Checklist

	STUDENT NAMES								
SCHOOL:									
TEACHER: **SCHOOL YEAR:**									

Mark: + = Mastery
√ = Satisfactory
− = Needs Improvement

LEVEL OF LANGUAGE PROFICIENCY (1–5)

MATH OBJECTIVES
• Add and subtract money amounts.
• Compare and order numbers to 1,000.
• Identify place value for each digit for numbers to 1,000.
• Count, read, write, and represent numbers to 1,000.
• Identify number patterns.
• Regroup ones or tens to add three-digit numbers.

ESL/TESOL LISTENING/SPEAKING
Connect new information to information previously learned.
Listen to and imitate how others use English.
Negotiate and manage interaction to accomplish tasks.
Participate in full class, group, and pair discussions.
Practice new language.
Use context to construct meaning

ESL/TESOL READING
Read about subject matter information.
Apply basic reading comprehension skills.
Follow written directions, implicit and explicit.

ESL WRITING
Write to demonstrate comprehension.
Write using spelling patterns and targeted English vocabulary.

	Add Hundreds	Regroup Ones	Regroup Tens
Examples			
Describe			
Describe			

1 **Preproduction**
• Did children write the unit vocabulary?
• Did they copy the definitions?

2 **3** **Early Production and Speech Emergence**
• Did children label the tabs correctly?

4 **5** **Intermediate and Advanced Fluency**
• Did children write definitions fo[r] unit vocabulary?
• Did they use correct spelling and grammar?

Place value to the thousands	Compare and Order Numbers to 1,000	Order Sets of Numbers to 1,000
	Numbers to 1,000	

Planner

Fractions, Probability, Data, and Operations

Assessment
p. 159
• Assessment Checklist
• Foldables

LOG ON Visit **www.mmhmath.com**

Unit Activities	
• **Activity 1** Readiness Same Parts, ... p. 142	• **Activity 3** Game-Fraction Match, 143
• **Activity 2** Music Poll, p. 142	• **Activity 4** Frogs, Frogs, Frogs, p. 143

Lessons	Key Objectives	Vocabulary	Materials	Resources
READ TOGETHER "Rainbow Punch" pp. 140–141	**Math:** Identify fractional parts of a whole. **ESL/TESOL:** Goal 1, Standard 3.	before, delight, during, equal parts, favorite, first, last, measure, mix, pitcher		Graphic Organizer 3
UNIT WARM-UP Understanding Fractions p. 144	**Math:** Identify fractional parts of a whole. Compare fractions. **ESL/TESOL:** Goal 2, Standard 1.	equal parts, fraction, greater than >, less than < , unequal parts	markers, paper shapes: circles, rectangles, squares, triangles	**Overhead Manipulative:** Fraction Strips
LESSON 1 Fractions pp. 146–147	**Math:** Identify fractional parts of a whole. Identify fractions as part of a group. **ESL/TESOL:** Goal 1, Standard 3.	equal parts, fraction	counters, shapes divided in halves, thirds, fourths, etc.	
LESSON 2 Probability pp. 148–149	**Math:** Identify the likelihood of events to occur. Make predictions. **ESL/TESOL:** Goal 2, Standard 1.	certain, equally likely, impossible, less likely, most likely, prediction, probable	colored cubes, clear plastic bags, index cards	Learning Resource 36
LESSON 3 Range, Mode, and Median pp. 150–151	**Math:** Identify range, mode, and median. **ESL/TESOL:** Goal 2/2, Standard 2/3.	median, mode, range	index cards, paper and pencils	Learning Resource 37
LESSON 4 Graphs pp. 152–153	**Math:** Read a coordinate graph. Read, use, and interpret line graphs. **ESL/TESOL:** Goal 2, Standard 2.	coordinate graph, line graph	paper and pencils	Learning Resource 38
LESSON 5 Multiplication pp. 154–155	**Math:** Use repeated addition and arrays to multiply. **ESL/TESOL:** Goal 1/2, Standard 3/2.	array, equal group, multiply, skip-count	counters	Learning Resource 39 Teacher Tool 10
LESSON 6 Division pp. 156–157	**Math:** Use repeated subtraction to divide. Divide to find equal shares. **ESL/TESOL:** Goal 2, Standard 2.	divide, equal share	cubes	Learning Resource 40
PROBLEM SOLVING p. 158 • Skill: Draw Conclusions • Strategy: Use a Pattern	Use skills and strategies to solve problems.			**Math Center Cards 7A, 7B**

See **Math at Home Family Guide** for additional math vocabulary, activities, and games in English, Spanish, and Haitian Creole.

English Vocabulary

Dear Family: Please help your child practice the key vocabulary words for this unit.

certain one of the choices will definitely happen

impossible an outcome is impossible to happen, if it is not given as a choice

likely an event that might take place

median the number that falls in the middle of numbers in order from least to greatest

mode the number that occurs most often in a list of data

prediction to tell what is going to happen before it happens

probability the chances or likelihood that something will happen

range the difference between the largest and smallest numbers in a list of data

unlikely the choices are such that there is only a slim chance that a particular choice will happen

Vocabulario en español

Estimados familiares: Por favor ayuden a su hijo/a a practicar las palabras del vocabulario de esta unidad.

seguro una de las opciones va a ocurrir definitivamente

imposible no es posible que un suceso ocurra si no es una opción

probable con buena posibilidad de que ocurra

mediana número en el medio dentro de un conjunto de datos en orden numérico

moda el número que aparece con mayor frecuencia en una lista de datos

predicción decir lo que va a pasar antes de que ocurra

probabilidad posibilidad de que suceda algo

rango diferencia entre el mayor y el menor número en un grupo de datos

improbable que es poco probable que ocurra ese suceso

Vokabilè an kreyol

Chè paran: Tanpri ede pitit la pratike mo vokabilè nan seksyon sa a.

sèten si youn nan chwa yo ap rive kanmèm

enposib yon rezilta enposib pou rive, si li pa prezante tankou yon chwa

pwobab yon evènman ki kapab rive

medyàn se nonb ki tonbe nan mitan nonb ki òdone depi piti pou rive nan pi gran

mòd se nonb ki parèt pi souvan nan yon seri done

prediksyon se lè w di yon evènman pral rive anvan evènman an rive

pwobablite se chans oswa posiblite pou yon evènman rive

etandi se diferans ant pi gran nonb ak pi piti nonb lan nan yon seri done

enpwobab se chwa ki montre gen ti chans tou piti pou yon chwa patikilye rive

© Macmillan/McGraw-Hill

Rainbow Punch

 30 minutes

Math Objectives
- Identify fractional parts of a whole.

ESL/TESOL Descriptor
- Listen to and imitate how others use English.

Reading Skill
- Sequence of events

Vocabulary
apple, before, club soda, cranberry, delight, during, equal parts, favorite, first, grape, juice, last, measure, mix, pitcher, punch, rainbow, recipe, seltzer, servings, sweet

Before Reading

Build Background/Oral Language
Explain that you will read a poem about how to make Rainbow Punch. Ask: **What is a rainbow?** Elicit from children that a rainbow has many different colors. Discuss that punch is a drink of two or more fruit juices.

During Reading

- Read the poem through once and invite children to ask about new or difficult words.
- Reread the poem line by line, inviting children to repeat each line after you. Have children name the juices and their colors. Ask: **How much of each kind of juice is in the recipe?** ($\frac{1}{4}$ cup)
- Read poem with the class in unison.

Phonological/Phonemic Awareness
Draw attention to the initial consonant clusters /sp/ in sparkling, /sw/ in sweet, /gr/ in grape, and /cr/ in cranberry. Have children repeat each word after you.

After Reading

Ask the class to help you write the sequence of events when making Rainbow Punch. Begin with what happens last—drinking the punch—and elicit events that led up to it. Ask questions such as **What happened before that? What happened first?** You may want to use Sequence of Events from Graphic Organizer 3. Ask children to write things that happened before making the punch, while making the punch, and after making it.

Cultural Link Invite children to discuss what fruit juices from their native countries they could use for a punch.

Art Ask children to use fraction words to make up their own punch recipe. Invite them to name and illustrate their recipes.

Assessment

Observe children's participation as you read the poem. See Assessment Checklist on page 159.

Multilevel Strategies

1 Preproduction
Direct children's attention to the picture of a measuring cup. Say: **Point to the $\frac{1}{4}$ cup line.**

Writing Ask children to write the fraction.

2 3 Early Production and Speech Emergence
Point to the picture of the measuring cup. Ask: **How much apple juice is in the Rainbow Punch recipe?**
Writing Ask children to write how much apple juice is in the recipe.

4 5 Intermediate and Advanced Fluency
Say: **Your friend wants the recipe for Rainbow Punch. What do you say?**

Writing Ask children to write the recipe for Rainbow Punch.

Rainbow Punch

Team up with a partner to measure and mix
Four equal parts it takes to fix.
It's an old favorite, this sparkling delight
Our Rainbow Punch so sweet and light.

Mix together in a pitcher to make two servings and ENJOY…

$\frac{1}{4}$ cup of apple juice

$\frac{1}{4}$ cup of grape juice

$\frac{1}{4}$ cup of cranberry juice

$\frac{1}{4}$ cup of seltzer or club soda

Activities

Readiness

ACTIVITY 1

INDIVIDUAL

Same Parts, Different Wholes

YOU NEED

inch graph paper

- Choose 2 boxes that are side by side. Draw a line around them. Now shade in one of the 2 boxes. That is how to show $\frac{1}{2}$. Write $\frac{1}{2}$ in the shaded box.

- Now choose 3 boxes that are side by side. Draw a line around them. Shade in one of the 3 boxes. That is how to show $\frac{1}{3}$. Write $\frac{1}{3}$ in the shaded box.

- Next, show $\frac{1}{4}$ and $\frac{1}{6}$.

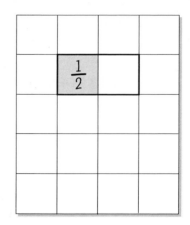

Identify Fractional Parts of a Whole

ACTIVITY 2

INDIVIDUAL

Music Poll

YOU NEED

The Poll Results show what 1,500 people said about their favorite kind of music.

Choose a different method for each problem.

Pencil/Paper

Mental Math

Calculator

1. How many more people like rock than jazz?

2. What is the total number of fans of folk and new age music?

3. How many classical and country fans are there altogether?

See answers on page 193.

Use Strategies and Skills to Solve Problems

Poll Results
classical 236
jazz 342
rock 408
folk 218
country 180
new age 89

Game Zone

ACTIVITY 3

PARTNERS

Fraction Match

Take turns.

YOU NEED
8 picture cards
8 fraction cards

- Turn over two cards. If the fraction and the picture match, keep the cards. If the cards do not match, turn them back over.

- Play until all the cards are matched. The person with the most cards wins.

Identify Fractions

ACTIVITY 4

SMALL GROUP

Frogs, Frogs, Frogs

◯ logs were in the pond.

There were ☐ frogs on each.

How many frogs in all?

Take turns.

YOU NEED
(5–9)
 (1–3)

- Spin a number for the circle.
  Roll a number for the square.
  The group solves the problems by drawing a picture.

- Write new problems using your own words. Solve them together.

Word List
branches
lily pads
flies
spiders

Use Repeated Addition to Multiply

Understanding Fractions

30 minutes

▶ **Key Strategy**
Use visuals

▶ **Format**
Whole class and small groups

▶ **Math Vocabulary**
equal parts, fraction, greater than >, less than <, unequal parts

▶ **Daily Vocabulary**
fourths, half, halves, same size, sixths, thirds, whole

▶ **Resource**
Overhead Manipulative

▶ **Materials**
markers, paper shapes including whole square; 3 squares divided into halves, quarters, and sixths; circles, rectangles, squares, triangles

Math Objectives	ESL/TESOL Descriptors
■ Identify fractional parts of a whole. ■ Compare fractions.	■ Participate in full class, group, and pair discussions. ■ Use context to construct meaning.

Activate Prior Knowledge Hand out circle "cookies" to pairs. Ask: *How can you share the cookie so each person has an* **equal part?** Elicit that they can cut the cookie in half. Fold one circle into 2 **unequal** parts and another into equal parts to show the difference between equal and unequal parts. Invite children to draw a line to divide their cookie into 2 equal parts. Ask: *How can you share the cookie with 4 children?* Elicit that they can cut the cookie into 4 equal parts. Have children fold their circles into fourths and draw another line dividing the cookie into 4 equal parts.

Hands-on Lesson

● Display a whole square and 3 squares divided into 2 equal parts, 4 equal parts, and 6 equal parts respectively. Ask children to identify the whole square. Point to the square divided in two and ask: *How many parts are there? Are they equal?* Tell children we use **fractions** to name the parts of a whole.

● Shade in one part of the square, and explain how to write a fraction for the shaded part. Say: *Write the number of shaded parts on top. Write the number of equal parts on the bottom.* Write $\frac{1}{2}$ on the shaded part. Repeat this exercise with the other squares, demonstrating the fractions $\frac{1}{4}$ and $\frac{1}{6}$.

● Have children compare the fractions. Ask: *Which is greater?* $\frac{1}{4}$ *or* $\frac{1}{2}$? $\frac{1}{2}$ *or* $\frac{1}{6}$? *Which fraction is less than* $\frac{1}{2}$? and so on. Write number sentences on the board. Then demonstrate how to show larger fractions, such as $\frac{3}{4}$ and $\frac{2}{6}$. You may wish to use **Overhead Manipulative:** Fraction Strips.

● Give pairs a variety of shapes and ask them to use their markers to divide them into 2, 4, or 6 equal parts.

● Ask them to color in some of the parts on each shape and work together to write the fraction for each one. Have children take turns reading the fractions.

Multilevel Strategies

1 Preproduction
Hold up a circles divided into equal parts. Ask: *Is this circle divided into equal parts?*

2 3 Early Production and Speech Emergence
Hold up the two circles one at a time and ask: *Are these parts equal?*

4 5 Intermediate and Advanced Fluency
Hold up the two circles one at a time and ask: *Are these parts equal? How do you know?*

Visit **www.mmhmath.com** to find printable **Vocabulary Cards** that help build academic language.

Procedure: Help children make these Foldables to write vocabulary words and definitions throughout the unit. Encourage children to use the Foldables as a study guide.

Matchbooks

1. Fold a sheet of 11" × 17" paper in half like a hamburger, leaving one side 1" longer than the other side.

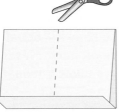

2. Fold the 1" tab forward over the short side.

3. Fold in half like a hamburger and cut along the fold line to form two Matchbooks.

4. Write fractions on the front tabs.

5. Write information about the fractions and their values under the tabs.

Going Further Children can use their Matchbooks to review by comparing their pictures and examples of fractions, unit fractions, unit fractions of a group, or other fractions of a group.

Pocket Book

1. Provide each child with a sheet of $8\frac{1}{2}$" × 11" paper.

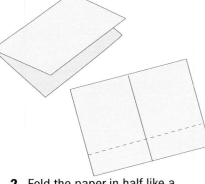

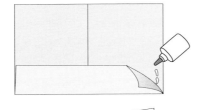

2. Fold the paper in half like a hamburger. Open and fold up a 2" tab along the long edge of the paper.

3. Glue the ends to form two pockets and label as illustrated.

4. As you work through the lessons, have children record information they learn on index cards or quarter-sheets of paper.

5. Sort and store the study cards in the pockets of the Pocket Book.

Going Further Children can use their Pocket Books to review by comparing their pictures and examples of repeated addition, using arrays to multiply, repeated subtraction, division, and using patterns.

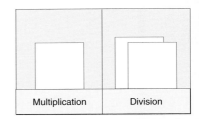

Multiplication   Division

Lesson 1

45 minutes

▶ **Key Strategy**
Use visuals

▶ **Format**
Whole class and student pairs

▶ **Math Vocabulary**
equal parts, fraction

▶ **Daily Vocabulary**
fourths, groups, halves, part, thirds, total, whole

Materials
- prepared shapes (circle, octagon, pentagon, rectangle, square, triangle) divided into halves, thirds, fourths, fifths, sixths, and eighths
- red and yellow counters

Assessment

Check children's mastery of the lesson vocabulary by observing them coloring parts to show a fraction. See page 159 for Assessment Checklist. Remind children to work on their Foldables.

Home Connection

Invite children to look for objects at home that can be divided into fractional parts. Ask them to make a list to share with the class.

Fractions

Math Objectives	**ESL/TESOL Descriptors**
■ Identify fractional parts of a whole. ■ Identify fractions as part of a group.	■ Practice new language. ■ Negotiate and manage interaction to accomplish tasks.

Activate Prior Knowledge Draw a circle that has 4 equal parts, a square that has three equal parts, and a rectangle that has two equal parts. Also draw a circle divided into two unequal parts and square divided into four unequal parts. Ask: *Which shape shows 4 equal parts? Which shape shows 2 equal parts? Which shape shows 3 equal parts?* Invite volunteers to identify each correct shape. Then ask: *Which shapes show unequal parts?*

Hands-on Lesson Remind children we use **fractions** to name equal parts of a whole. Point to the circle and say: *This is one whole. It has four equal parts.*

- Ask a child to shade 1 part of the circle divided into fourths. Say: *The shaded part is 1 part of 4 equal parts.* Model how to write a fraction. Say: *I write the number of the shaded parts on top. I write the total number of equal parts on the bottom.*

- Ask a child to shade two parts of the square divided into thirds. Ask: *What is the total number of equal parts? How many equal parts are shaded?* Write the fraction, saying *I can write 2 for the number of shaded parts and 3 for the total number of equal parts.*

- Now shade the entire square. Say: *I can write a fraction for the whole.* Write $\frac{3}{3}$ next to the square.

- Hand out a variety of shapes to pairs. Ask children to take turns choosing a shape, telling how many equal parts there are in all, and deciding how many parts to shade. The other child writes the fraction for the number of parts that have been colored and reads the fraction.

- Encourage pairs to continue this activity creating as many different fractions as they can with the shapes.

- Hand out octagons with drawn lines that show 8 equal parts to pairs. Have children cut the octagons apart and then put them back together. Then one child hides a random number of parts and challenges his or her partner to write a fraction for the missing parts. Encourage children to take turns until they have written as many fractions as they can.

- Hand out 5 red and 5 yellow counters to pairs. Invite them to share the counters equally between them. Ask: **How many counters do you each have?** Invite children to count out 8 counters and share them equally. Ask: **How many counters do you each have? How do you know that it is an equal share?** (each has the same number of counters)

- Point out to children that they have already learned how to use fractions to name a part of a whole but that we also use fractions to name a part of a group. Display 3 red counters and 3 yellow counters. Say: **There are two equal parts in this group. One part of the group is yellow and one part is red. I can write a fraction for the yellow part of this group. The fraction for the yellow part is $\frac{1}{2}$.** Write $\frac{1}{2}$ on the board.

- Display a group of 3 red counters, 3 yellow counters, and 3 yellow counters. Ask: **How many equal parts are there in this group of counters?** (3) **How many parts of the group are yellow?** (2 parts) **So I can write a fraction for the yellow part of this group.** Write $\frac{2}{3}$ on the board.

- Hand out counters to children, and work with them to make different groups for $\frac{1}{2}$, $\frac{1}{4}$, and $\frac{1}{3}$. Continue until children have reinforced the concept that the bottom number tells how many equal parts there are in the group.

You may want to use Fraction Strips from **Overhead Manipulatives** to reinforce children's understanding of fractions.

Challenge Ask children to work in pairs. Encourage them to draw a picture of 12 balloons, color a fraction of the balloons purple, and write the fraction. Extend the activity by inviting children to draw other pictures that show different fractions. Display children's drawings around the room.

Multilevel Strategies

1 **Preproduction**
Say: **Shade 1/3 of a circle**.

Writing Ask children to write the fraction for the shaded part of the circle. Encourage children to read it.

2 3 **Early Production and Speech Emergence**
Hold up a circle that has $\frac{1}{3}$ shaded and ask: **What fraction of the circle is shaded?**

Writing Ask children to write a sentence that tells how much of the circle is shaded.

4 5 **Intermediate and Advanced Fluency**
Ask: **How can you show $\frac{1}{3}$ of a circle?**

Writing Ask children to write sentences about what the numbers in $\frac{1}{3}$ represent.

 45 minutes

▶ **Key Strategy**
Use visuals

▶ **Format**
Whole class and student pairs

▶ **Math Vocabulary**
certain, equally likely, impossible, less likely, most likely, prediction, probable

▶ **Daily Vocabulary**
always, fewer, more, possible

▶ **Resource**
Learning Resource 36

Materials
• clear plastic bags
• cubes
• index cards labeled more likely, less likely, and equally likely

Assessment

Check children's mastery of the lesson vocabulary by observing them while making predictions. See page 159 for Assessment Checklist. Remind children to work on their Foldables.

Home Connection

Encourage children to toss a penny with a family member 10 times, predicting and recording the results to share with the class.

Probability

Math Objectives	**ESL/TESOL Descriptors**
■ Identify the likelihood of events to occur.	■ Negotiate and manage interaction to accomplish tasks.
■ Make predictions.	■ Practice new language.

Activate Prior Knowledge Display a clear bag with 10 purple cubes in it. Ask: *If you pick a cube, what color will it be? Will the cube always be purple?* (Yes, it is certain.) *How do you know?* (All the cubes are purple.)

Hands-on Lesson Prepare 3 clear bags with the following combinations: (1) 7 yellow and 1 purple cube; (2) 4 yellow and 4 purple cubes; and (3) 6 yellow and 2 purple cubes. Hold up bag (1). Invite a child to pick a cube without looking. Ask: *What color are you most likely to pick? Why?*

● Hold up bag (2). Invite a child to pick a cube without looking. Ask: *What color are you less likely to pick? Why?*

● Hold up bag (3). Invite a child to pick a cube. Ask: *Are you equally likely to choose a yellow or purple cube? Why?*

● Hand out bags of cubes and Learning Resource 36 to pairs. Tell children they will take turns picking a cube 10 times. Ask them to **predict** the color they will pick most often and to record their **prediction.**

● Have children shake the bag. Ask one child to pick a cube without looking and put a tally mark next to the appropriate color on the worksheet. Tell children to return the cube to the bag and shake it. Then the other partner takes a turn, until each partner has had 5 turns. Ask each pair to compare their results with another pair and then report the results to the class.

Challenge Invite pairs to create their own cube combinations and questions to exchange with another pair.

Multilevel Strategies

1 Preproduction
Hold up a bag with 8 yellow cubes and 1 purple cube. Say: *Point to or say the color you are most likely to pick.*

Writing Ask children to write the color of the cube that they are most likely to pick.

2 3 Early Production and Speech Emergence
Hold up a bag with 8 yellow cubes and 1 purple cube. Ask: *What color are you most likely to pick?*

Writing Ask children to write a sentence that tells what color they are most likely to pick.

4 5 Intermediate and Advanced Fluency
Hold up a bag with 8 yellow cubes and 1 purple cube. Ask: *Which color are you most likely to pick? Why?*

Writing Ask children to write sentences about the cubes using the vocabulary words.

Name _____

Probability

1. Our Prediction

What color do you think you are most likely to pick? _____

Why? _____

COLOR	TALLY MARK
Green	
Orange	
Yellow	

2. Our Results

What color did you pick most often? _____

3. Comparing Results

We compared our results with _____

When we compared our results, we found _____

_____

_____

_____

_____

Lesson 3

45 minutes

▶ **Key Strategy**
Use visuals

▶ **Format**
Whole class and student pairs

▶ **Math Vocabulary**
median, mode, range

▶ **Daily Vocabulary**
appears, describe, greatest, least, middle, most often, set of numbers

▶ **Resource**
Learning Resource 37

Materials
• index cards
• paper and pencil

Assessment

Check children's mastery of the lesson vocabulary by observing them as they complete the lesson. See page 159 for Assessment Checklist. Remind children to work on their Foldables.

Home Connection

Invite children to ask a family number to name five favorite numbers. Ask children to find the range and mode of the numbers and report the results to the class.

Range, Mode, and Median

Math Objective	ESL/TESOL Descriptors
■ Identify range, mode, and median.	■ Listen to, speak, read, and write about subject matter information. ■ Use context to construct meaning.

Activate Prior Knowledge Write these numbers on separate index cards: *8, 24, 8, 12,* and *3*. Put them in a pile and ask children to put the set of numbers in order from greatest to least. Ask: **Which number do you see more than once?**

Hands-on Lesson Write these numbers on the board: *8, 5, 2, 5,* and *5.* Tell children we can learn different things about a set of numbers. These things include the **range**, the **mode**, and the **median**. Write words on chalkboard or flash cards

● Explain how to find the range. Say: **First, find the greatest number.** (8) Say: **Next, find the least number.** (2) **Last, we subtract the least number from the greatest number.** ($8 - 2 = 6$) **The range for this set of numbers is 6.**

● Explain how to find the mode. Say: **The mode is the number we see most often in the set. The mode for this set of numbers is 5.**

● Explain how to find the median. Say: **The median is the number in the middle.** Have children look at the set of numbers on the board, and ask a volunteer to cross out the greatest number and the least number. Repeat until only one number is left. (5)

● Hand out Learning Resource 37 and ask children to work in pairs to complete the worksheet.

Challenge Hand out 7 random number cards from 1–20 to pairs. Ask them to write the set of numbers and work together to find the range, mode, and median.

Multilevel Strategies

1 Preproduction
Write: *6, 3, 4, 4,* and *2.*
Ask: **What is the mode for this set of numbers?**

Writing Ask children to write the numbers they can use to find the range of this set of numbers.

2 3 Early Production and Speech Emergence
Write: *6, 3, 4, 4,* and *2.*
Ask: **What is the mode for this set of numbers?**

Writing Ask children to write the number sentence for finding the range of this set of numbers.

4 5 Intermediate and Advanced Fluency
Write: *6, 3, 4, 4,* and *2.*
Ask: **How can we find the mode for this or any other set of numbers?**

Writing Ask children to explain how to find the range of a set of numbers.

Name _____

Data Daze!

Use the data in the table to answer the questions.

1. What is the greatest number and the least number?

   _____ and

   _____

2. Write the number sentence to find the range. (greatest number − least number =)

   _____

OUR FAVORITE NUMBERS!	
Name	**Number**
Josie	14
Oscar	7
Luke	12
Maya	5
Lucia	7

3. What is the range? _____

4. Which number is the mode? _____
   (Mode is the number you see most often)

Find the **median** of this set of numbers: 8, 6, 11, 4, 12
Remember…

1. Order the numbers from least to greatest.

   _____

2. Then cross out the greatest number and the least number.

3. Cross out the greatest number and the least number again.

4. The number that is left is the median. _____

Lesson 4

 45 minutes

▶ **Key Strategy**
Use visuals

▶ **Format**
Whole class and student pairs

▶ **Math Vocabulary**
coordinate graph, line graph

▶ **Daily Vocabulary**
compare, data, information, right, start, unit, up

▶ **Resource**
Learning Resource 38

Materials
- bar graph
- paper and pencils

Assessment

Check children's mastery of the lesson vocabulary by observing them as they create graphs. See page 159 for Assessment Checklist. Remind children to work on their Foldables.

Home Connection

Have children take home the Learning Resource to share. Invite children to show a family member how to mark a dot where the goats live at on the coordinate grid.

Graphs

Math Objectives	**ESL/TESOL Descriptors**
■ Read a coordinate graph.	■ Compare and contrast information.
■ Read, use, and interpret line graphs.	■ Represent information visually and interpret information.

Activate Prior Knowledge Display a bar graph. Ask children what they know about the different ways we can show data (bar graph, chart, table, picture graph). Ask children what they can learn by looking at the bar graph.

Hands-on Lesson Hand out Learning Resource 38. Identify the **coordinate graph.** Explain we use coordinate graphs to show where things are. Point out the 2 zeros at the corner, the numbers that go to the right, and the numbers that go up.

- Point and say: *Start at (0, 0) and count 4 units to the right. Now count up 1 unit.* Ask: *What animal is at (4, 1)?* (*rabbit*) Say: *Let's find the goat. Count the units to the right until you reach the line where the goat is. Then count the units that go up to find the goat. Where is the goat?* (*1, 2*)

- Continue by asking children to find the animals at (1, 3) (*horse*) and (4, 2) (*pig*). Ask: *What numbers tell the location of the cow and the duck?*

- Point to the chart and **line graph**. Say: *We can use a line graph to compare data over time.* Read the chart data. Say: *We can use this data to make a line graph.* Ask: *How much did Newton weigh at 3 years?* (*9 lbs*) Then point to the dot for Newton's weight at 3 years on the line graph.

- Work with children to plot the graph. Then have them connect the dots to make a line graph. Discuss the completed graphs.

Challenge Have pairs create two questions about the data on the line graph. Then have them exchange questions with another pair and answer them.

Multilevel Strategies

1 Preproduction
Display a coordinate graph of the farmyard. Ask: *Is the pig on coordinates (4, 2)?*

Writing Say: *Write the numbers that tell where the horse is.* (*1, 3*)

2 3 Early Production and Speech Emergence
Display a coordinate graph of the farmyard. Ask: *What animal is at 4, 2?* (*pig*)

Writing Ask children to write the name of the animal at 1, 3. (*horse*)

4 5 Intermediate and Advanced Fluency
Display a coordinate graph of the farmyard. Ask: *How can we find the animal that is at 4, 2?*

Writing Ask children to write the steps for finding the location of the horse.

Name _____

Fun with Graphs!

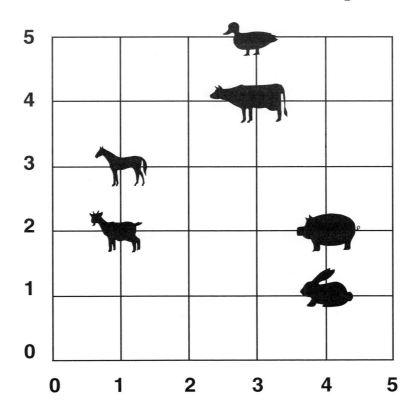

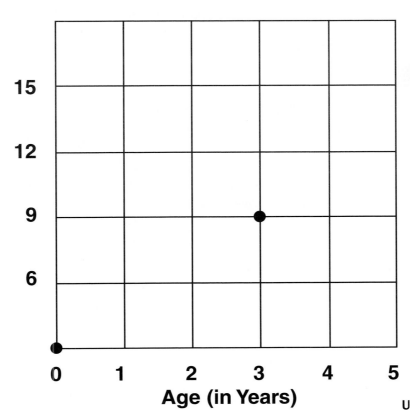

NEWTON'S WEIGHT	
Age	Weight
1 yr	6 pounds
2 yrs	9 pounds
3 yrs	9 pounds
4 yrs	12 pounds
5 yrs	15 pounds

Age (in Years)

45 minutes

▶ **Key Strategy**
Use manipulatives

▶ **Format**
Whole class and student pairs

▶ **Math Vocabulary**
array, equal group, multiply, skip-count

▶ **Daily Vocabulary**
repeated, rows

▶ **Resources**
Learning Resource 39
Teacher Tool 10

Materials
• counters

Assessment

Check children's mastery of the lesson vocabulary by observing them as they complete the lesson. See page 159 for Assessment Checklist. Remind children to work on their Foldables.

Home Connection

Have children work with a family member to make equal groups of objects like straws and draw a picture to share with the class.

Multiplication

Math Objective	**ESL/TESOL Descriptors**
■ Use repeated addition and arrays to multiply.	■ Use context to construct meaning. ■ Demonstrate knowledge through application.

Activate Prior Knowledge Draw a number line between 0–12 on the board. Invite children to **skip-count** by twos as you draw lines to show each "skip." Repeat by skip-counting by threes and fours. Explain to children that knowing how to skip-count can help them learn to multiply.

Hands-on Lesson Explain there are different ways to find the total if we are counting an equal number of items in groups. Hand out 20 counters to pairs. Invite them to put the counters into **equal groups** with four counters in each group. Ask: *How many groups of 4 do you have?* (5)

- Say: *We can skip-count to find the total.* Skip-count by fours to 20 in unison. Say: *We can also use addition.* Write $4 + 4 + 4 + 4 + 4 = 20$. Then point out to the children that they can also **multiply** to find the total. Say: *We have 5 equal groups of 4, so we can also write a multiplication sentence.* Write $5 \times 4 = 20$.

- Repeat this activity asking children to put the counters into equal groups with five counters in each group. (5, 10, 15, 20 or $5 + 5 + 5 + 5 = 20$) Say: *We have 4 equal groups of 5, so we can multiply.* Write $4 \times 5 = 20$. Then hand out Learning Resource 39 for children to complete.

- Hand out Teacher Tool 10: 5 x 5 grid. Tell children they can use an **array** to help them multiply. Say: *There are 5 rows in this array. Put 3 counters in each row. How many counters are there in all?* Write: $3 + 3 + 3 + 3 + 3 = 15$ and $5 \times 3 = 15$ on the board. Repeat this activity several times.

Challenge Hand out 30 counters to pairs. Challenge them to make as many arrays as they can to show 12 and then write a multiplication sentence for each array.

Multilevel Strategies

1 Preproduction
Say: *Use counters to make three equal groups of four*.

Writing Ask children to write the number that tells how many equal groups there are.

2 3 Early Production and Speech Emergence
Use counters to display 3 groups of 4 on a table. Ask: *How many equal groups are there?*

Writing Ask children to write a number sentence to find the total.

4 5 Intermediate and Advanced Fluency
Display 3 groups of 4 counters. Ask: *What are three ways to find how many there are?*

Writing Ask children to write how they use arrays.

Name _____

Star Stories

Add. Then multiply.

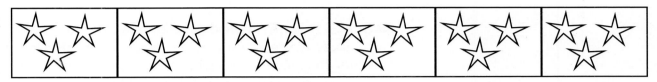

1. ___ + ___ + ___ + ___ + ___ + ___ = ___

   ___ × ___ = ___

2. ___ + ___ + ___ + ___ = ___

   ___ × ___ = ___

3. ___ + ___ + ___ + ___ + ___ = ___

   ___ × ___ = ___

▶ **Key Strategy**
Use manipulatives

▶ **Format**
Whole class and student
pairs

▶ **Math Vocabulary**
divide, equal share

▶ **Resource**
Learning Resource 40

Materials
• cubes

Assessment

Check children's mastery of the
lesson vocabulary by observing
them as they complete the
lesson. See page 159 for
Assessment Checklist. Remind
children to work on their
Foldables.

Home Connection

Ask children to work with a
family member to draw a picture
of a group of objects divided
into equal shares to share with
the class.

Division

Math Objectives	**ESL/TESOL Descriptors**
■ Use repeated subtraction to divide.	■ Demonstrate knowledge through application in a variety of contexts.
■ Divide to find equal shares.	■ Use context to construct meaning.

Activate Prior Knowledge Draw a number line from 0–12. Invite children to
count back by twos with you as you draw lines to show the "skips" between the
numbers. Repeat by counting back by threes and fours. Explain to children that
counting back can help them learn to **divide**.

Hands-on Lesson Explain there are two ways to separate objects into equal
groups. Give pairs 12 connected cubes. Ask them to separate the cubes into
groups of 3. Ask: **How many equal groups do you have?** (4)

• Say: **We can also use subtraction to find the number of equal groups.** Model how
to use repeated subtraction to find the number of equal groups. Say: **First we
write the total number of cubes.** (12) **Then we subtract by 3.** Write these number
sentences under one another: $12 - 3 = 9; 9 - 3 = 6; 6 - 3 = 3; 3 - 3 = 0$.
Then I count how many times I subtracted. (4) Have children repeat each
subtraction sentence with you and count how many times you subtracted.

• Repeat this activity with groups of four. Say: **We have 3 equal groups of 4. We can
use subtraction.** Write: $12 - 4 = 8; 8 - 4 = 4; 4 - 4 = 0$.

• Say: **We can also write a division sentence to find the number of equal groups.
We have 12 counters. There are 4 in each group.** Write $12 \div 4 = 3$. Repeat this
activity several times. Then hand out Learning Resource 40: Party Time! for
children to complete.

Challenge Have children draw a picture that shows dividing to find **equal shares**.

Multilevel Strategies

❶ Preproduction
Say: **Use 8 counters to
make equal groups
of 2.**

Writing Write: $8 - 2 = 6$,
$6 - 2 = 4$, $4 - 2 = 2$,
$2 - 2 = 0$. Ask children to
write the number of times
you subtracted 2.

**❷❸ Early Production
and Speech Emergence**
Write: $8 - 2 = 6$, $6 - 2 = 4$,
$4 - 2 = 2$, $2 - 2 = 0$. Ask:
**What number did I
subtract? How many
times?**

Writing Ask children to
write how many groups of
2 are in 8.

**❹❺ Intermediate
and Advanced Fluency**
Ask: **How can we find the
number of equal groups
of 2 in 8?**

Writing Ask children to
write the division sentence
that shows how many
groups of 2 are in 8.

Name _____

Party Time!

Divide. Draw a picture to help.

1. 10 birthday hats
2 equal groups
How many hats in each group?

$10 \div 2 =$ _____

2. 16 ice cream cones
4 equal groups
How many ice cream cones in each group?

$16 \div 4 =$ _____

3. 12 cookies
4 equal groups
How many cookies in each group?

$12 \div 4 =$ _____

4. 25 balloons
5 equal groups
How many balloons in each group?

$25 \div 5 =$ _____

Problem Solving
Reading for Math

Read → Plan → Solve → Look Back

Remind students of
the basic steps
of problem solving.

SKILL: Draw Conclusions

Model the skill using a word problem such as the following:

1 Dani and Carol are in a reading club. They both read the same number of pages every day. At the end of the week they tell each other about the books they read. This week Dani read 6 books and Carol read 4. Explain.

2 I know that they read the same number of pages. I know that Dani read more books than Carol. I have to ask myself questions to figure out why.

3 **Think:** What did they do that is the same? They read the same number of pages. The books are not the same length. The books Carol read must be longer.

4 Does my answer make sense? Yes. How do I know? If they read the same number of pages, then there must be more pages in the books Carol read.

Distribute **Math Center Card 7A** to children.

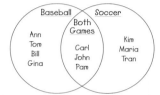

Math Center Card 7A

Reading for Math Skill

DRAW CONCLUSIONS • USE A DIAGRAM

PARTNERS

Work with a partner.

1. Gina and her friends play baseball and soccer. Look at the diagram.

Baseball Soccer
Both Games
Ann
Tom
Bill
Gina
Carl
John
Pam
Kim
Maria
Tran

2. Answer each question. Use the diagram.
- How many students play baseball but not soccer?
- How many students play soccer but not baseball?
- Which students like to play both games?
- Do more students play baseball or soccer?

Math Center Card, Grade 2, Unit 7, 7A

STRATEGY: Use a Pattern

Model the strategy using a word problem such as the following:

Read How many fingers are on 7 children?

Plan I know there are 10 fingers on 1 child.
I can find a pattern.
I can make a chart to show the pattern.

Solve I can carry out my plan.
There are 70 fingers on 7 children.

Look Back What pattern did I see? I counted by tens.
Does my answer make sense? Yes.

Distribute **Math Center Card 7B** to children.

Math Center Card 7B

Problem Solving: Strategy

USE A PATTERN • MULTIPLYING

INDIVIDUAL

Write 3 more multiplication sentences for each pattern. Describe each pattern.

1. $4 \times 1 = 4$
   $4 \times 2 = 8$
   $4 \times 4 = 16$

2. $3 \times 1 = 3$
   $3 \times 2 = 6$
   $3 \times 3 = 9$

3. $6 \times 1 = 6$
   $6 \times 2 = 12$
   $6 \times 3 = 18$

4. Write your own multiplication pattern.

Math Center Card, Grade 2, Unit 7, 7B

Assessment Checklist

	STUDENT NAMES										
SCHOOL:											
TEACHER: **SCHOOL YEAR:**											
Mark: + = Mastery ✓ = Satisfactory – = Needs Improvement											
LEVEL OF LANGUAGE PROFICIENCY (1–5)											
MATH OBJECTIVES											
• Divide to find equal shares.											
• Identify fractional parts of a whole.											
• Identify fractions as part of a group.											
• Compare fractions.											
• Identify the likelihood of events to occur.											
• Identify range, mode, and median.											
• Read, use, and interpret line graphs.											
ESL/TESOL LISTENING/SPEAKING											
Use context to construct meaning.											
Negotiate and manage interaction to accomplish tasks.											
Listen to, speak, read, and write about subject matter information.											
Compare and contrast information.											
Demonstrate knowledge through application in a variety of contexts.											
ESL/TESOL READING											
Read about subject matter information.											
Apply basic reading comprehension skills.											
Follow written directions, implicit and explicit.											
ESL WRITING											
Write to demonstrate comprehension.											
Write using spelling patterns and targeted English vocabulary.											

❶ Preproduction
- Did children write the unit vocabulary?
- Did they copy the definitions?

❷❸ Early Production and Speech Emergence
- Did children label the tabs correctly?
- Did they write the vocabulary words?
- Did they copy the definitions?

❹❺ Intermediate and Advanced Fluency
- Did children write definitions for the unit vocabulary?
- Did they use correct spelling and grammar?

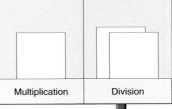

Glossary

add (+)

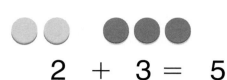

$$2 + 3 = 5$$

$$\begin{array}{r} 2 \\ +3 \\ \hline 5 \end{array}$$

addend

$$\begin{array}{r} 31 \\ +18 \\ \hline 49 \end{array}$$

31 ← addend
+18 ← addend

after

47 48 49

48 is after 47.

A.M.

the hours from
midnight to noon

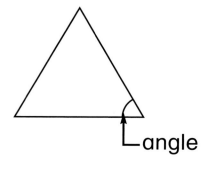

It is 7:00 A.M.

angle

angle

area

The area of this
rectangle is
6 square units.

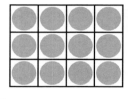

array

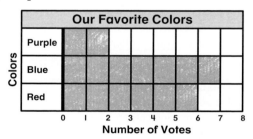

$$3 \times 4 = 12$$

bar graph

Our Favorite Colors

Colors								
Purple								
Blue								
Red								

0 1 2 3 4 5 6 7 8
Number of Votes

before

47 48 49

47 is before 48.

between

47 48 49

48 is between 47 and 49.

calendar

This is a calendar for September.

September						
S	M	T	W	T	F	S
				1	2	3
4	5	6	7	8	9	10
11	12	13	14	15	16	17
18	19	20	21	22	23	24
25	26	27	28	29	30	

chart

Favorite Sports	
Soccer	7
Basketball	5
Football	4
Baseball	2

capacity

the amount a container holds when filled

circle

cent (¢)

I¢   I cent

compare

  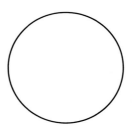

5 is less   6 is equal   8 is greater
than 7.   to 6.   than 4.

centimeter (cm)

I cm

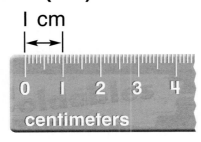

cone

certain

An event will definitely happen.

It is certain that you will pick a .

congruent

same size and same shape

© Macmillan/McGraw-Hill

coordinate graph

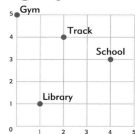

count back

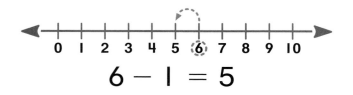

$$6 - 1 = 5$$

count on

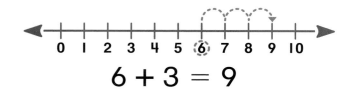

$$6 + 3 = 9$$

counting pattern

2, 4, 6, 8, 10, 12, 14	Counting by 2s
3, 6, 9, 12, 15, 18, 21	Counting by 3s
5, 10, 15, 20, 25, 30, 35	Counting by 5s

cube

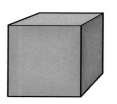

cup (c)

cylinder

data

information that is
collected for a survey

decimal point

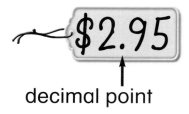

decimal point

degrees Celsius (°C)

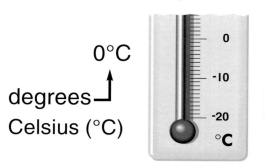

0°C

degrees
Celsius (°C)

degrees Fahrenheit (°F)

16°F

degrees ⌐
Fahrenheit (°F)

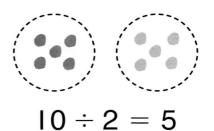

difference

$17 - 9 = 8$

$$\begin{array}{r} 17 \\ -\ 9 \\ \hline 8 \end{array}$$

difference ⟶ 8

Subtract to find the difference.

digit

any single figure used when representing a number

354

3, 5, and 4 are digits in 354.

dime

10¢   10 cents

distance

the space between two points

The distance between the
2 houses is 200 yards.

divide

$10 \div 2 = 5$

dollar ($)

$1.00   100 cents

doubles

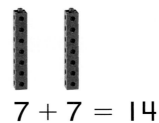

$7 + 7 = 14$

doubles plus 1

$7 + 8 = 15$

edge

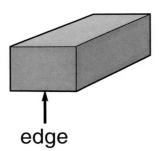

edge

© Macmillan/McGraw-Hill

equal groups

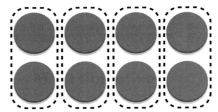

There are 4 equal groups of counters.

equal parts

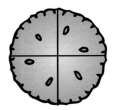

This pie is cut into 4 equal parts.

equal share

Two children can share these crayons equally.

equally likely

Without looking, it is equally likely that you will pick a ▧ as a ■.

estimate

47 + 22

50 + 20

about 70 ◄——— estimate

even

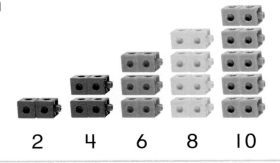

2   4   6   8   10

expanded form

another way of writing a number

364

300 + 60 + 4 ◄——— expanded form

face

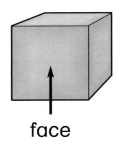

face

fact family

$$5 + 6 = 11 \qquad 11 - 6 = 5$$
$$6 + 5 = 11 \qquad 11 - 5 = 6$$

flip

a mirror image of a figure

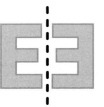

fluid ounce (fl oz)

8 fluid ounces in a cup

foot (ft)

12 inches = 1 foot

fraction

| $\frac{1}{2}$ | $\frac{1}{3}$ | $\frac{1}{4}$ | $\frac{3}{4}$ |

gallon (gal)

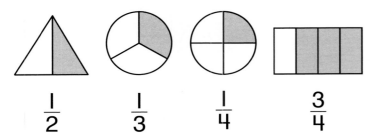

4 quarts = 1 gallon

half dollar

50¢   50 cents

half hour

30 minutes = half hour

hexagon

6 sides and 6 angles

hour

60 minutes = 1 hour

hour hand

hour hand

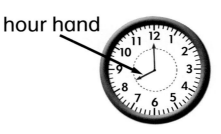

hundreds

234

↑
2 hundreds

impossible

an event that cannot happen

It is impossible to pick a 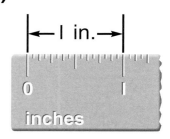.

inch (in.)

is equal to (=)

35 is equal to 35.

35 = 35

is greater than (>)

36 is greater than 35.

36 > 35

is less than (<)

35 is less than 36.

35 < 36

key

tells you what each symbol stands for

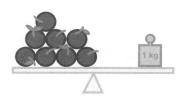

kilogram (kg)

1 kilogram is about 8 apples.

length

Length is how long something is.

less likely

Without looking, it is less likely that you will pick a .

line graph

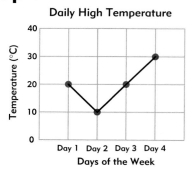

line of symmetry

a line on which a figure can be folded so that its two halves match exactly

line plot

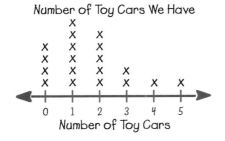

liter (L)

There are 1,000 milliliters in 1 liter.

make a ten

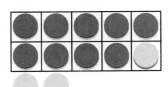

$10 + 2$

Make a ten to add $9 + 3$.

measure

to find length, weight, capacity, or temperature

median

the middle number when numbers are put in order from least to greatest

6 7 8 9 10

The median is 8.

meter (m)

1 meter = 100 centimeters

1 meter is a little longer than a baseball bat.

milliliter (mL)

This medicine dropper holds about 1 milliliter.

minute

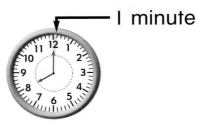

1 minute

60 seconds = 1 minute

minute hand

minute hand

missing addend

$$9 + \boxed{} = 14$$

The missing addend is 5.

nickel

5¢   5 cents

mode

the number that occurs
most often in a set of data

4   7   10   36   7   2

The mode is 7.

number line

month

This calendar
shows the month
of September.

September						
S	M	T	W	T	F	S
				1	2	3
4	5	6	7	8	9	10
11	12	13	14	15	16	17
18	19	20	21	22	23	24
25	26	27	28	29	30	

number sentence

$$6 + 8 = 14 \text{ or } 14 = 6 + 8$$

more likely

Without looking, it is more likely
that you will pick a ▦.

odd

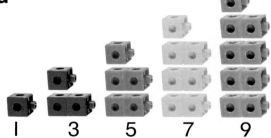

1   3   5   7   9

multiply

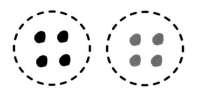

$$2 \times 4 = 8$$

ones

3 ones

ordinal numbers

numbers used to tell position

first   second   third

perimeter

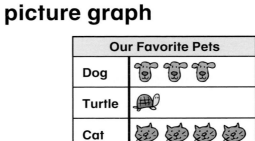

the distance around a shape

ounce (oz)

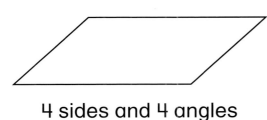

One CD weighs about 1 ounce.

pictograph

Favorite Birds	
Crow	☺
Robin	☺ ☺ ☺ ☺
Jay	☺ ☺ ☺ ☺ ☺ ☺

Key: Each ☺ stands for 2 votes.

parallelogram

4 sides and 4 angles

picture graph

Our Favorite Pets	
Dog	🐶 🐶 🐶
Turtle	🐢
Cat	🐱 🐱 🐱 🐱

penny

1¢   1 cent

pint (pt)

2 cups = 1 pint

pentagon

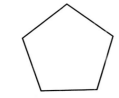

5 sides and 5 angles

place value

the amount that each digit in a number stands for

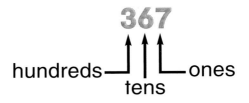

hundreds — tens — ones

P.M.

the hours from
noon to midnight

It is 11:00 P.M.

pound (lb)

The book weighs about
1 pound.

prediction

a telling that something
will happen

probable

an event that is more likely to happen

It is probable that you will pick a .

pyramid

quadrilateral

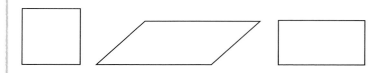

4 sides and 4 angles

quart (qt)

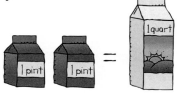

2 pints = 1 quart

quarter

25¢   25 cents

quarter hour

quarter hour = 15 minutes

range

the difference between the least
number and the greatest number

4   7   10   36   7   2

greatest   least

36 − 2 = 34. The range is 34.

reasonable

A reasonable answer makes sense.

$$19 + 32 = 51$$

$$20 + 30 = 50$$

51 is a reasonable answer.

round

to find the ten or hundred closest to a number

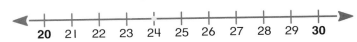

24 rounded to the nearest ten is 20.

rectangle

4 sides and 4 angles

rule

Add 3 is the rule.

Rule: Add 3

In	Out
10	13
20	23
30	33

rectangular prism

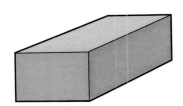

side

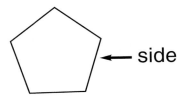

← side

regroup

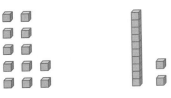

12 ones = 1 ten 2 ones

skip-count

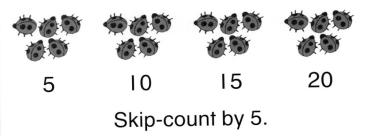

| 5 | 10 | 15 | 20 |

Skip-count by 5.

related facts

$$5 + 1 = 6$$
$$1 + 5 = 6$$

slide

to move a figure horizontally, vertically, or diagonally

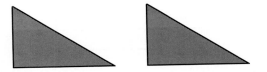

sphere

square

4 sides and 4 angles

subtract (−)

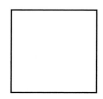

$$5 - 3 = 2$$

sum

sum
↓
$$3 + 2 = 5$$

The sum of 3 plus 2 is 5.

survey

a way to collect data

Favorite Sports	
Soccer	卌 ‖
Basketball	卌
Football	‖‖‖
Baseball	‖

This survey shows favorite sports.

tally mark

a mark used to record data

$$| = 1 \qquad 卌 = 5$$

temperature

a measure of hot or cold

The temperature is 79°F.

tens

6 tens

thousands

1,253

1 thousand

trapezoid

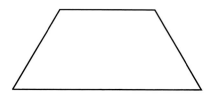

4 sides and 4 angles

© Macmillan/McGraw-Hill

172 Glossary

triangle

3 sides and 3 angles

turn

a figure that is rotated around a point

unit

The things that repeat in
a pattern make a unit.

vertex

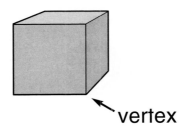

vertex

week

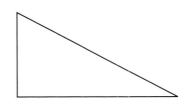

week →

There are 7 days in a week.

yard

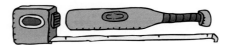

3 feet = I yard

year

Jan | Feb | Mar | Apr
May | Jun | Jul | Aug
Sep | Oct | Nov | Dec

one year

Teacher Tool

Name _____

Number Cards, 0–9

4	9
3	8
2	7
1	6
0	5

Name _____

Number Cards, 10–20

15

14

13

12

11

10

20

19

18

17

16

Name_____

Number Cards, by Tens

10 20 30 40 50

60 70 80 90 100

Name _____

10-Frame

Name _____

Number Lines: Blank; to 12; by Tens

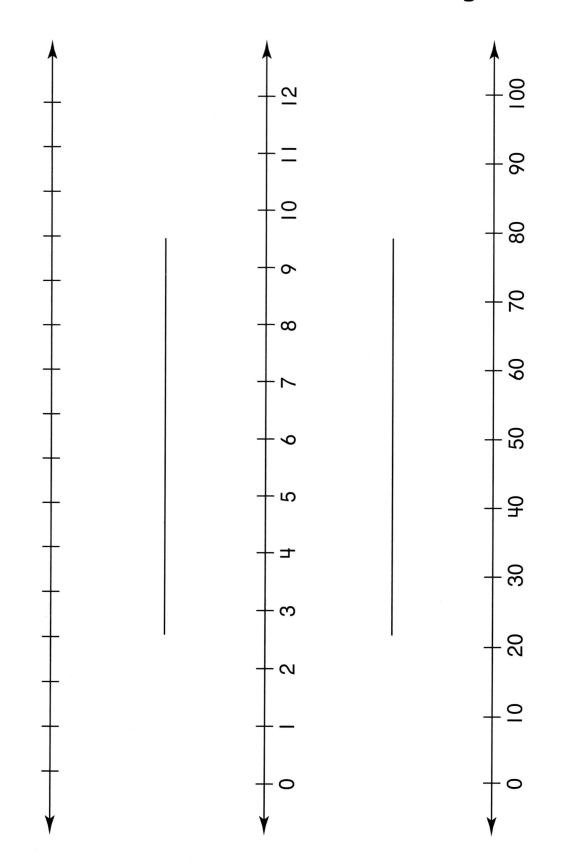

Name _____

Place-Value Models

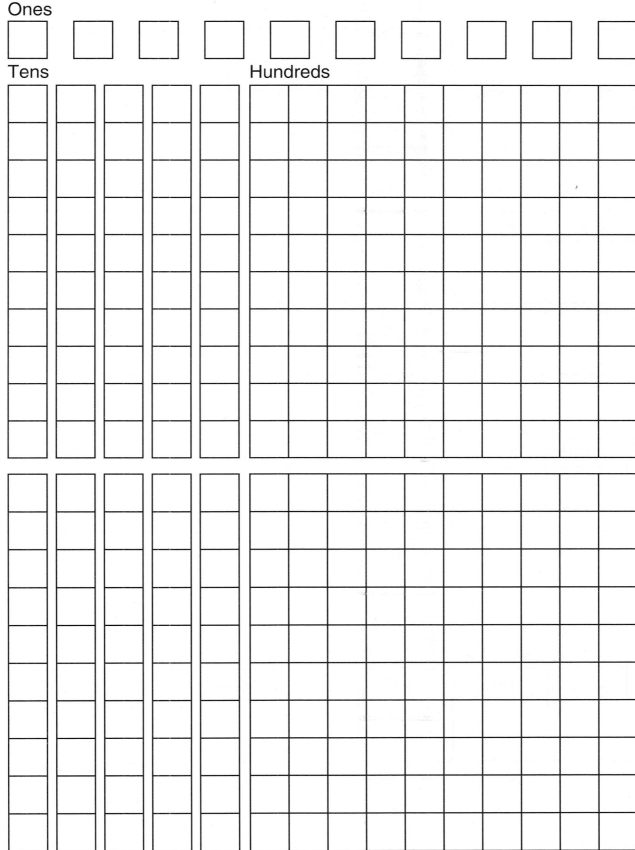

Ones

Tens   Hundreds

Name _____

Short Place-Value Charts

tens	ones

tens	ones

tens	ones

_____   _____   _____

tens	ones

tens	ones

tens	ones

_____   _____   _____

hundreds	tens	ones

hundreds	tens	ones

_____   _____

hundreds	tens	ones

hundreds	tens	ones

_____   _____

Name _____

Place-Value Workmat (2-Digit)

Name _____

Inch Graph Paper

Name

1$\frac{1}{4}$-Inch Grid Paper (5 x 5 Square)

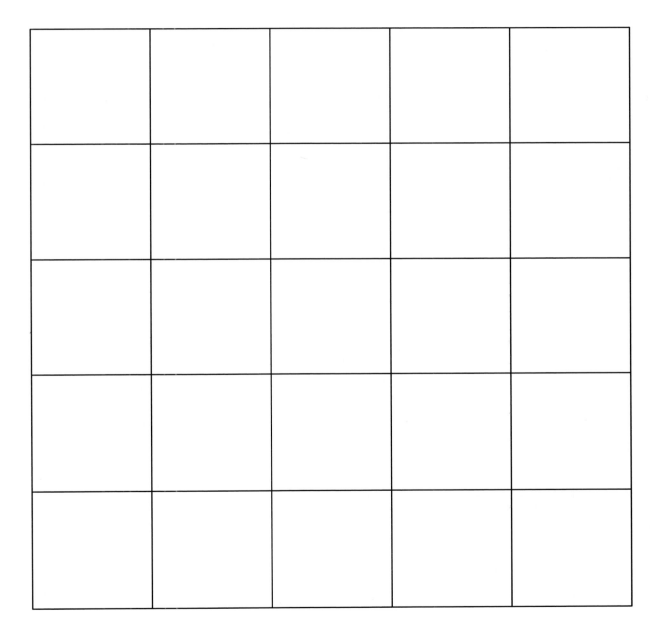

Name _____

Centimeter Graph Paper

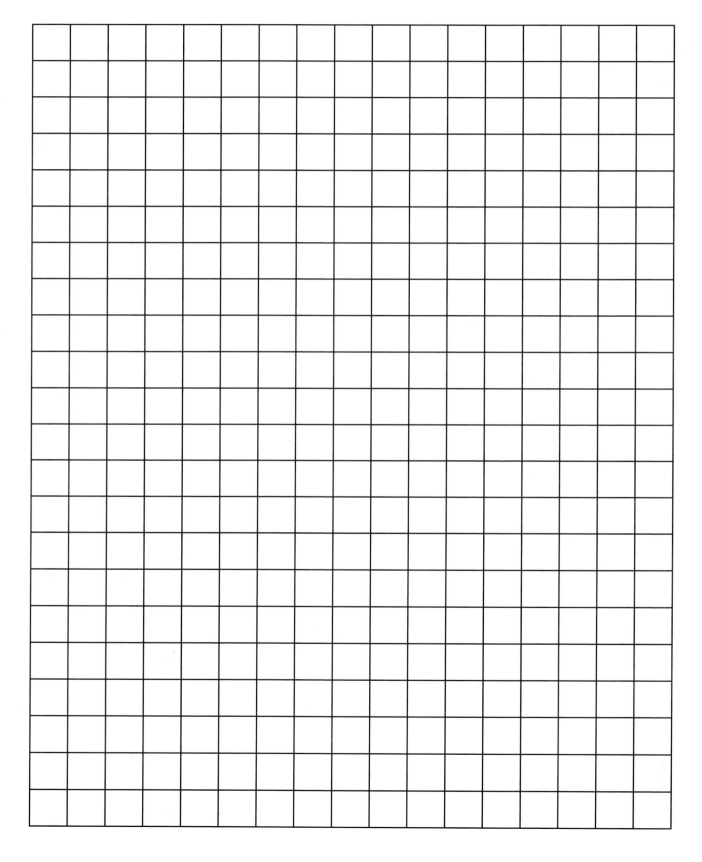

Teacher Tool

Name _____

Centimeter Dot Paper

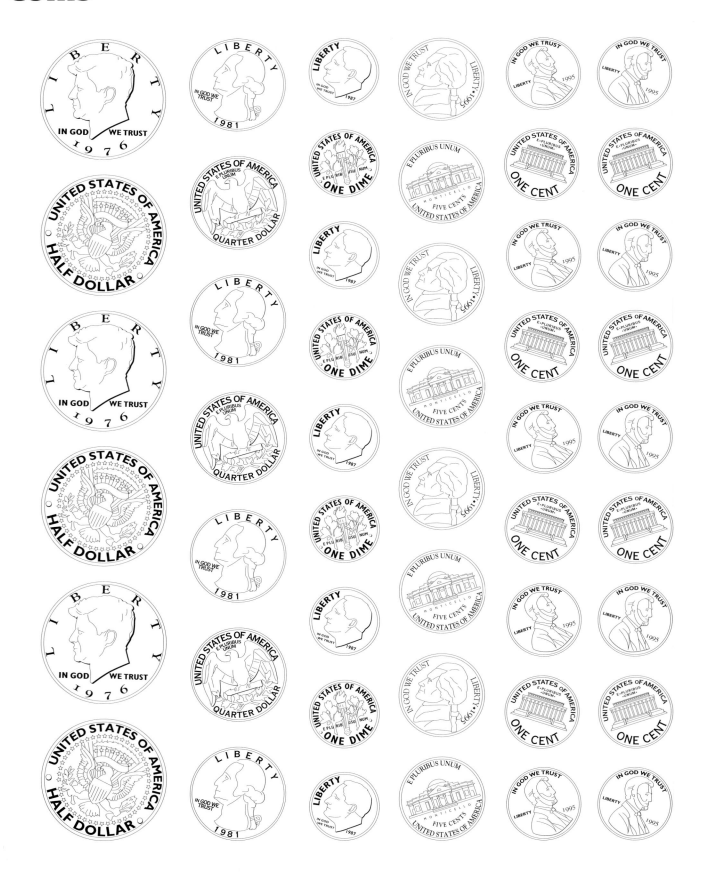

Teacher Tool

Name

Coins

Name

Bills

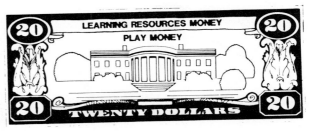

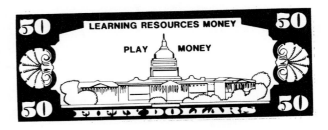

Name

Analog Clockface

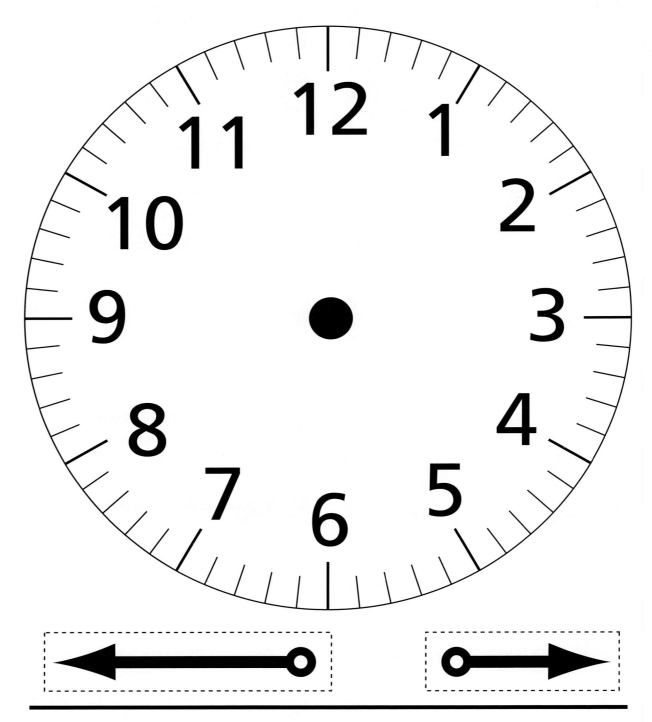

1. Mount on heavy paper.
2. Cut out the clock hands.
3. Attach them to the clock with a paper fastener.

Name

Clock Cards with Times

Name

Clock Cards without Times

Name _____

Calendar

Sunday	Monday	Tuesday	Wednesday	Thursday	Friday	Saturday

Teacher Tool

Centimeter Rulers

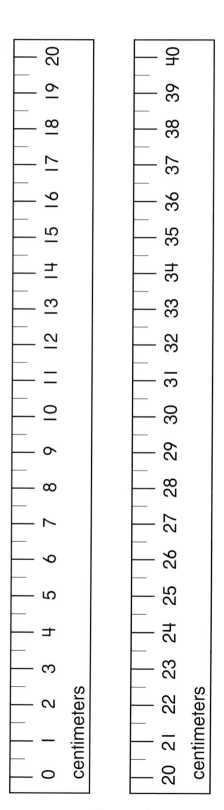

1. Cut strips out.   2. Tape together to form a metric ruler.

Name _____

Thermometers: Celsius, Fahrenheit

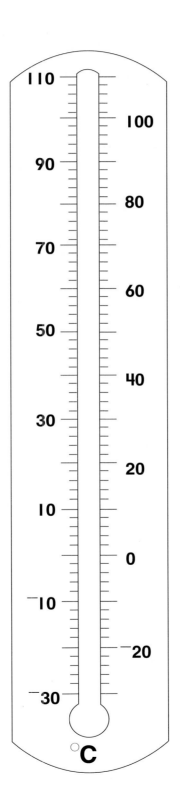

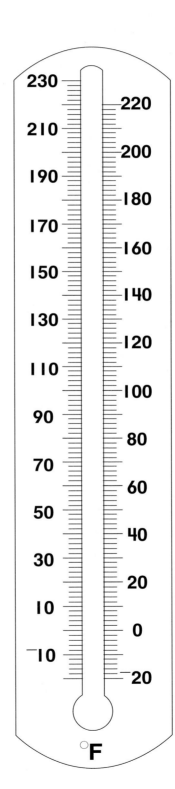

Graphic Organizer

Word Web

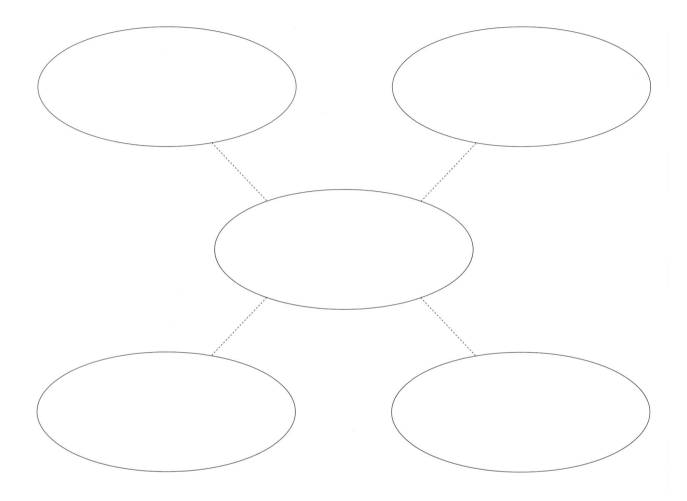

Graphic Organizer

Four-Column Chart

Graphic Organizer

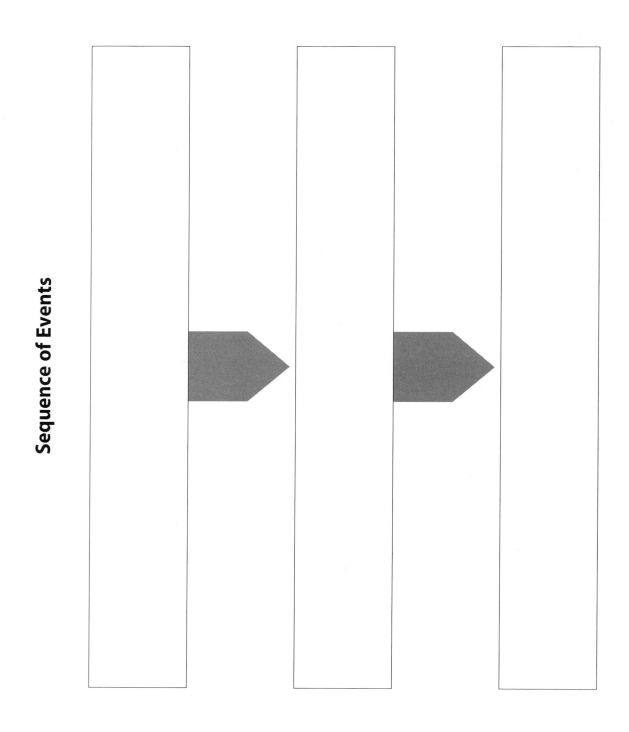

Sequence of Events